Prayers

Prayers
Michel Quoist

translated by Agnes M. Forsyth
and Anne Marie de Commaille

AVON
PUBLISHERS OF BARD, CAMELOT AND DISCUS BOOKS

KV: *The Holy Bible*, trans. by Ronald Knox. Copyright 1944, 1948 and 1950, Sheed and Ward, Inc., New York. Quoted with the permission of His Eminence, the Cardinal of Westminster. Other Scripture excerpts are from: *The New English Bible, New Testament.* © The Delegates of the Oxford University Press 1961. Reprinted by permission.

AVON BOOKS
A division of
The Hearst Corporation
959 Eighth Avenue
New York, New York 10019

Translated from *Prières* by Michel Quoist;
Paris, Les Editions Ouvrieres, 1954
Copyright © 1963 by Sheed & Ward, Inc.
Library of Congress Catalog Card Number: 63-17141
ISBN: 0-380-42614-5

First Avon Printing, August, 1975
Fourth Printing

AVON TRADEMARK REG. U.S. OFF. AND IN
OTHER COUNTRIES, MARCA REGISTRADA, HECHO EN
U.S.A.

Printed in the U.S.A.

CONTENTS

Introduction: *To Pray These Pages*   ix

If we knew how to listen to God   1
    I Like Youngsters   3
    Son, I Beseech You, Don't Sleep Any More   6

If only we knew how to look at life   11
    I Would Like to Rise Very High   13

All life would become a sign   17
    The Telephone   19
    Green Blackboards   20
    The Wire Fence   21
    My Friend   22
    The Brick   23
    The Baby   24
    Posters   25
    The Subway   26
    The Swing   27
    At the Door   28

All of life would become prayer   29
    Prayer Before a Twenty-Dollar Bill   31
    The Pornographic Magazine   34
    The Tractor   38

The Funeral   40
The Sea   44
Eyes   47
To Love: the Prayer of the Adolescent   51
I Found Marcel Alone   54
The Delinquent   57
Thank You   61
The Priest: A Prayer on Sunday Night   64
I Spoke, Lord   69
That Face, Lord, Haunts Me   72
Hunger   77
Housing   81
The Hospital   84
He Was in the Middle of the Street   87
The Bald Head   90
Football at Night   93
Lord, I Have Time   96
There Are Two Loves Only   100
All   105

Stages of the Road   109
Lord, Deliver Me from Myself   111
Lord, Why Did You Tell Me to Love?   116
Help Me to Say "Yes"   120
Nothing, I Am Nothing. . . .   124
Agony: Lord, I Am Crushed   127
Temptation   131
Sin   134
It Is Dark   138
Lord, You Have Seized Me   141
Before You, Lord   145

Prayers on the Way of the Cross   149
  (I). Jesus Is Condemned to Death   151
  (II). Jesus Bears His Cross   153
  (III). Jesus Falls for the First Time   155
  (IV). Jesus Meets His Mother   157
  (V). Simon of Cyrene Helps Carry Jesus' Cross   159
  (VI). A Woman Wipes the Face of Jesus   161
  (VII). Jesus Falls for the Second Time   163
  (VIII). Jesus Rebukes the Daughters of Jerusalem   165
  (IX). Jesus Falls for the Third Time   167
  (X). Jesus Is Stripped of His Garments   169
  (XI). Jesus Is Nailed to the Cross   171
  (XII). Jesus Dies on the Cross   173
  (XIII). Jesus Is Given to His Mother   176
  (XIV). Jesus Is Laid in the Tomb   178

INTRODUCTION
To Pray These Pages

Before being written, these pages were both lived and prayed. They stem from the lives of committed Christians offered day by day to God. We record these experiences to help others bring to God every aspect of their lives and to transfigure their lives through prayer. All the facts mentioned here are authentic.

These pages can hardly be used as "set prayers" in the usual sense. They are meditations on life, designed to help Christians discover the riches of a contact with God arising from the daily events of their existence. But they must not make us neglect the liturgy or the words which were put on our lips first by Christ himself, and then by the Church.

God always initiates his dialogue with man. That is why, in the first chapters, we have attempted to speak for God, as Péguy did before us.

But very soon the Christian must do more than imagine what God is saying to him; he must listen to him actually speaking in his life and in the world. God addresses us through every event, even the most insignificant. Very short prayers, of which we have given a few samples, may help us to meet the Lord at every step on our road.

Yet it is not only when active that we must turn to God. We must learn to be still before him and talk over our lives fully with him—like a child who has been away for a while and returns to tell his father in detail of all that has happened. Some of our longer prayers describe this intimate sharing with our Father; they begin with an object, a person, an event, and throw the light of faith on some part of our everyday life. In these prayers there is a constant call to give ourselves to men, our brothers. Wherever the Father has placed us, there we must strive that his kingdom of love and justice may come. This is not a matter of choice; it is the very meaning of our Christian life.

Some Christians may be disturbed by certain of these prayers. We beg them not to skip over the troublesome pages, not to shut off questions God asks through them. It is better to listen to God summoning us in this life than to hear him condemning us in the next.

Prayer often reveals the extent both of our self-giving to others and of our friendship with Christ. We have grouped together prayers which, we hope, will enlighten Christians on their road—obscure at times—toward total self-giving.

Further, those who love the God who has surrendered himself for them must follow him on his way to Calvary. However, we have suffered too much from (and sometimes smiled at) the well-worn phrases of our parents' "Stations of the Cross" not to attempt re-writing them very simply here. We know that our words, too, will quickly lose their force. That is unimportant. The cut flower fades, but others grow.

Naturally, one should not read this book as one would a novel. Purposely varied, these prayers are meant to respond to the situations that the Christian encounters and help him to weave them into his prayer.

Finally, we have prefaced the prayers with texts of Scripture, to give the Christian, if he did not have it already, the desire to meditate on the Gospels and to find in them his daily nourishment. Thus are united here, supplementing each other, the Gospel and life, the two channels through which God speaks to men.

May those who read these pages hear God and answer him. In writing them, we hope for one thing only: to prepare the reader for the amazing dialogue between man and his God.

MICHEL QUOIST

Le Havre, June 18, 1954

If we knew
how to listen to God

If we knew how to listen to God, we would hear him speaking to us. For God does speak. He speaks in his Gospels. He also speaks through life—that new gospel to which we ourselves add a page each day. But we are rarely open to God's message, because our faith is too weak and our life too earthbound. To help us listen, at the beginning of our new intimacy with Christ, let us imagine what he would say if he himself interpreted his Gospels for the men of our day.

I LIKE YOUNGSTERS

"They brought children for him to touch; and the disciples scolded them for it. But when Jesus saw this he was indignant, and said to them, 'Let the children come to me; do not try to stop them; for the kingdom of God belongs to such as these. I tell you, whoever does not accept the kingdom of God like a child will never enter it.'" (Mark X, 13-15)

God says: I like youngsters. I want people to be like them.
I don't like old people unless they are still children.
I want only children in my Kingdom; this has been decreed from
    the beginning of time.
Youngsters—twisted, humped, wrinkled, white-bearded—all
    kinds of youngsters, but youngsters.
There is no changing it; it has been decided. There is room for
    no one else.

I like little children because my image has not yet been dulled
    in them.
They have not botched my likeness; they are new, pure, without a
    blot, without a smear.
So, when I gently lean over them, I recognize myself in them.

I like them because they are still growing, they are still improving.

They are on the road, they are on their way.

But with grown-ups there is nothing to expect any more.

They will no longer grow, no longer improve.

They have come to a full stop.

It is disastrous—grown-ups thinking they have arrived.

I like youngsters because they are still struggling, because they are still sinning.

Not because they sin, you understand, but because they know that they sin, and they say so, and they try not to sin any more.

But I don't like grown-ups. They never harm anyone; they have nothing to reproach themselves for.

I can't forgive them; I have nothing to forgive.

It is a pity, it is indeed a pity, because it is not true.

But above all, I like youngsters because of the look in their eyes. In their eyes I can read their age.

In my heaven, there will be only five-year-old eyes, for I know of nothing more beautiful than the pure eyes of a child.

It is not surprising, for I live in children, and it is I who look out through their eyes.

When pure eyes meet yours, it is I who smile at you through the flesh.

But on the other hand, I know of nothing sadder than lifeless eyes in the face of a child.

The windows are open, but the house is empty.

Two eyes are there, but no light.

4

And, saddened, I stand at the door, and wait in the cold and
  knock. I am eager to get in.
And he, the child, is alone.
He gets stout, he hardens, he dries up, he gets old. Poor old
  fellow!

Alleluia! Alleluia! Open, all of you, little old men!
It is I, your God, the Eternal, risen from the dead, coming to
  bring back to life the child in you.
Hurry! Now is the time. I am ready to give you again the beauti-
  ful face of a child, the beautiful eyes of a child.
For I love youngsters, and I want everyone to be like them.

SON, I BESEECH YOU,
DON'T SLEEP ANY MORE

We must contemplate Christ on the way to Calvary. We must relive with him the stations of his Cross to become deeply aware of his love for us. But his Passion is not fully completed. Lived by the Christ who assumed all the sins and sufferings of men two thousand years ago, it is now relived in the world, and will be till the end of time. Christ, living in his members, continues to suffer and die for us under our eyes. The Way of the Cross winds through our towns and cities, our hospitals and factories, and through our battlefields; it takes the road of poverty and suffering in every form.

It is before these new stations of the Cross that we must stop and meditate and pray to the suffering Christ for strength to love him enough to act.

"It is now my happiness to suffer for you. This is my way of helping to complete, in my poor human flesh, the full tale of Christ's afflictions still to be endured, for the sake of his body which is the church." (Colossians I, 24)

"I shall be in agony till the end of time," God says.
I shall be crucified till the end of time.
My sons the Christians don't seem to realize it.
I am scourged, buffeted, stretched out, crucified; I die in front
    of them and they don't know it. They see nothing; they are
    blind.
They are not true Christians, or they would not go on living
    while I am dying.

Lord, I don't understand; it is not possible, you exaggerate.
I would defend you if you were attacked.
I would be at your side if you were dying.
Lord, I love you!

That is not true, God says. Men are deluding themselves.
They say they love me, they believe they love me, and, as I am
    willing to admit, they are often sincere; but they are terribly
    mistaken. They do not understand, they do not see.
Slowly everything has been distorted, dried up, emptied.
They think they love me because once a month they honor my
    Sacred Heart;
As if I loved them only twelve times a year!
They think they love me because they keep to their devotions
    regularly, attend Benediction, eat fish on Fridays, burn a
    candle or say a prayer before a picture of my Sacred Heart.

But I am not made of plaster, God says, nor of stone, nor of
    bronze.
I am living flesh, throbbing, suffering.
I am among men, and they have not recognized me.
I am poorly paid, I am unemployed, I live in a slum, I have

7

tuberculosis, I sleep under bridges, I am in prison, I am oppressed, I am patronized.

And yet I said to them: "Whatever you do to my brothers, however humble, you do to me." That's clear.

The terrible thing is that they know it, but don't take it seriously.

"They have broken my heart," God says, "and I have waited for someone to have pity on me, but no one has."

I am cold, God says, I am hungry, I am naked.

I am imprisoned, laughed at, humiliated.

But this is a minor passion, for men have invented more terrible ordeals.

Armed with their liberty, formidably armed with their liberty,

They have invented. . . .

"Father, forgive them; they know not what they do."

They have invented war, actual war.

And they have invented the Passion, a worse one.

For I am everywhere that men are, God says,

Since the day when I slipped among them, on a mission to save them all,

Since the day when I definitely committed myself to trying to gather them together.

Now I am rich and I am poor, a workman and a boss.

I am a union man and a non-union man, a striker and a strike breaker, for men—alas!—make me do all kinds of things.

I am on the side of the demonstrators and on the side of the police, for men—alas!—transform me into a policeman.

I am a leftist, a rightist, and even in the center.

I am on this side of the Iron Curtain and beyond it.

I am a German and a Frenchman, a Russian and an American,

A Chinese from Nationalist China and one from Communist China,

8

I am from Vietnam and from Vietminh.
I am everywhere men are, God says.

They have accepted me, they possess me, the traitors!
Hail, Master!
And now I am with them, one of them, their very selves.
Now, see what they have done to me. . . .
They are scourging me, crucifying me,
They tear me apart when they tear at one another.
They kill me when they kill one another.
Men have invented war. . . .
I jump on mines, I gasp my last breath in foxholes,
I moan, riddled with shrapnel; I collapse under the volley of
    machine-gun fire,
I sweat men's blood on all battlefields,
I cry out in the night and die in the solitude of battle.
O world of strife, immense cross on which, every day, men
    stretch me!
Wasn't the wood of Golgotha enough?
Was this immense altar necessary for my sacrifice of love?
While around me men keep on shouting, singing, dancing, and,
    as if insane, crucify me in an enormous burst of laughter.

Lord, enough! Have pity on me!
Not that! It is not I!

9

Yes, son, it is you.
You and your brothers, for
>   several blows are needed to drive in a nail,
>   several lashes are needed to furrow a shoulder,
>   several thorns are needed to make a crown,
>   and you belong to the humanity that all together condemns me,

It matters not whether you are among those who hit, or among those who watch; among those who do it or among those who let it happen.
You are all guilty, actors and spectators.
But above all, son, don't be one of those who are asleep, one of those who can still fall asleep . . . in peace. Sleep!
Sleep is terrible!
"Can you not watch one hour with me?"

On your knees, son! Do you not hear the roar of battle?
The bell is ringing,
Mass is starting,
Crucified by men,
God is dying for you.

10

If only we knew how to look at life

If only we knew how to look at life as God sees it, we would realize that nothing is secular in the world, that everything contributes to the building of the Kingdom of God. To have faith is not only to raise one's eyes to God to contemplate him; it is also to look at this world—with Christ's eyes.

If we had allowed Christ to penetrate our whole being, if we had purified ourselves, the world would no longer be an obstacle. It would be a perpetual incentive to work for the Father in order that, in Christ, his Kingdom might come on earth as it is in heaven.

We must pray to have sufficient faith to know how to look at life.

I WOULD LIKE
TO RISE VERY HIGH

"Praise be to the God and Father of our Lord Jesus Christ, who has bestowed on us in Christ every spiritual blessing in the heavenly realms. In Christ he chose us before the world was founded, to be dedicated, to be without blemish in his sight, to be full of love; and he destined us—such was his will and pleasure—to be accepted as his sons through Jesus Christ." (Ephesians I, 3-5)

"He has made known to us his hidden purpose—such was his will and pleasure determined beforehand in Christ—to be put into effect when the time was ripe: namely, that the universe, all in heaven and on earth, might be brought into a unity in Christ." (Ephesians I, 9-10)

I would like to rise very high, Lord;
Above my city,
Above the world,
Above time.
I would like to purify my glance and borrow your eyes.

★

I would then see the universe, humanity, history, as the Father
    sees them.
I would see in the prodigious transformation of matter,
In the perpetual seething of life,
Your great Body that is born of the breath of the Spirit.
I would see the beautiful, the eternal thought of your Father's
    Love taking form, step by step:
Everything summed up in you, things on earth and things in
    heaven.
And I would see that today, like yesterday, the most minute
    details are part of it.
Every man in his place,
Every group
And every object.
I would see a factory, a theatre, a collective-bargaining session
    and the construction of a fountain.
I would see a crowd of youngsters going to a dance,
A baby being born, and an old man dying.
I would see the tiniest particle of matter and the smallest throb-
    bing of life,
Love and hate,
Sin and grace.
Startled, I would understand that the great adventure of love,
    which started at the beginning of the world, is unfolding
    before me,
The divine story which, according to your promise, will be com-
    pleted only in glory after the resurrection of the flesh,
When you will come before the Father, saying: All is accom-
    plished. I am Alpha and Omega, the Beginning and the
    End.
I would understand that everything is linked together,
That all is but a single movement of the whole of humanity and

14

of the whole universe toward the Trinity, in you, by you, Lord.

I would understand that nothing is secular, neither things, nor people, nor events,

But that, on the contrary, everything has been made sacred in its origin by God

And that everything must be consecrated by man, who has himself been made divine.

I would understand that my life, an imperceptible breath in this great whole,

Is an indispensable treasure in the Father's plan.

Then, falling on my knees, I would admire, Lord, the mystery of this world

Which, in spite of the innumerable and hateful snags of sin,

Is a long throb of love towards Love eternal.

I would like to rise very high, Lord,
Above my city,
Above the world,
Above time.
I would like to purify my glance and borrow your eyes.

All life
would become a sign

If we knew how to look at life through God's eyes, we would see it as innumerable tokens of the love of the Creator seeking the love of his creatures. The Father has put us into the world, not to walk through it with lowered eyes, but to search for him through things, events, people. Everything must reveal God to us.

Long prayers are not needed in order to smile at Christ in the smallest details of daily life. The following lines attempt to give a few simple examples of the manifestations of his love.

THE TELEPHONE

I have just hung up; why did he telephone?
I don't know. . . . Oh! I get it. . . .

I talked a lot and listened very little.

Forgive me, Lord; it was a monologue and not a dialogue.
I explained my idea and did not get his;
Since I didn't listen, I learned nothing,
Since I didn't listen, I didn't help,
Since I didn't listen, we didn't commune.

Forgive me, Lord, for we were connected,
And now we are cut off.

GREEN BLACKBOARDS

The school is up-to-date.
Proudly the Principal enumerates all the improvements.
The finest discovery, Lord, is the green blackboards.
The scientists have studied the matter at length, they have made
    experiments;
We now know that green is the ideal color, that it doesn't tire
    the eyes, that it is quieting and relaxing.

It has occurred to me, Lord, that you didn't wait so long to paint
    the trees and the meadows green.
Your research laboratories were efficient, and in order not to tire
    us, you perfected a number of shades of green for your
    modern meadows.
And so the "finds" of men consist in discovering what you have
    thought from time immemorial.
Thank you, Lord, for being the good Father who gives his
    children the joy of discovering by themselves the treasures
    of his intelligence and love.
But keep us from believing that by ourselves we have invented
    anything at all.

20

THE WIRE FENCE

The wires are holding hands around the holes;
To avoid breaking the ring, they hold tight the neighboring
    wrist,
And it's thus that with holes they make a fence.

Lord, there are lots of holes in my life.
There are some in the lives of my neighbors.
But if you wish, we shall hold hands,
We shall hold very tight,
And together we shall make a fine roll of fence to adorn
    Paradise.

MY FRIEND

I shook hands with my friend, Lord,
And suddenly, when I saw his sad and anxious face, I feared
　　that you were not in his heart.
I am troubled, as I am troubled before a closed tabernacle when
　　where is no light to show that you are there.

If you were not there, Lord, my friend and I would be separated.
For his hand in mine would be only flesh in flesh
And his love for me that of man for man.
I want your life for him as well as for me.
For it is only in you that he can be my brother.

THE BRICK

The bricklayer laid a brick on the bed of cement.
Then, with a precise stroke of his trowel, spread another layer
And, without a by-your-leave, laid on another brick.
The foundations grew visibly,
The building rose, tall and strong, to shelter men.

I thought, Lord, of that poor brick buried in the darkness at
    the base of the big building.
No one sees it, but it accomplishes its task, and the other bricks
    need it.
Lord, what difference whether I am on the rooftop or in the
    foundations of your building, as long as I stand faithfully
    at the right place?

THE BABY

The mother left the carriage for a minute, and I went over to
    meet the Holy Trinity living in the baby's pure soul.
It was asleep, its arms carelessly laid on the embroidered sheet.
Its closed eyes looked inward and its chest gently rose and fell
As if to murmur: This dwelling is inhabited.

Lord, you are there.

I adore you in this little one who has not yet disfigured you.
Help me to become like him once more,
To recapture your likeness and your life now so deeply buried in
    my heart.

POSTERS

They are loud.
I cannot avoid them, for they crowd together on the wall, allur-
   ing and tempting.
Their violent colors hurt my eyes,
And I can't rid myself of their distasteful presence.

Lord, in the same way too often I draw attention to myself.
Grant that I may be more humble and unobtrusive,
And above all keep me from trying to impress others through
   showy display,
For it is your Light only, Lord, that must draw all men.

THE SUBWAY

The last ones squeeze in.
The door rolls shut.
The subway rumbles off.
I can't move;
I am no longer an individual but a crowd,
A crowd that moves in one piece like jellied soup in its can.

A nameless and indifferent crowd, probably far from you, Lord.
I am one with the crowd, and I see why it's sometimes hard for
    me to rise higher.
This crowd is heavy—leaden soles on my feet, my slow feet—a
    crowd too large for my overburdened skiff.
Yet, Lord, I have no right to overlook these people; they are
    my brothers,
And I cannot save myself, alone.

Lord, since you wish it, I shall head for heaven "in the subway."

THE SWING

He was gently swinging at the end of the ropes.
Eyes shut, relaxed and drifting, he listened to the murmur of
the breeze that sang a lullaby as it swayed him back and
forth.
And minutes floated away to the cadence of the swing.

So, Lord, I walk through the city as through a vast county fair,
and see men drifting, blown by the breezes of life.
Some smile, and yield to passing pleasures,
Others with taut faces curse the wind that shakes them and
knocks them into one another.

Lord, I want them to stand up on their swings,
I want them to grasp the cords that you hold out to them,
I want them to harden their muscles and brace their vigorous
bodies, and stamp on their lives the direction they have
chosen,

For you do not want your sons to drift,
But to live.

AT THE DOOR

The boy stumbled on the landing and the door slammed behind
    him.
He had been punished.
Suddenly aware of his disgrace, he rushed in anger at the un-
    feeling door.
He slapped it, pounded it, stamping and shrieking.
But on the wooden surface not a fiber moved.
The boy caught sight of the keyhole—ironic eye of that sullen
    door—
But on peering into it he saw that it was blocked.
Then, in despair, he sat down and cried.

I watched him, smiling, and realized, Lord, that often I exhaust
    myself before locked doors.
I want to make my points, convince, prove,
And I talk and brandish arguments,
I strike hard to reach the imagination or the emotions,
But I am politely or violently dismissed—I waste my strength,
    vain fool that I am.

Grant, Lord, that I may learn to wait reverently,
Loving and praying in silence,
Standing at the door till it is opened.

28

All of life would become prayer

If we knew how to listen to God, if we
knew how to look around us, our whole
life would become prayer. For it unfolds
under God's eyes and no part of it must be
lived without being freely offered to him.

At first we communicate with God
through words, which may be dispensed
with later on. Let us then make use of the
following pages, but soon discard words,
as one does the peelings of a fruit. Words
are only a means.

However, the silent prayer which has
moved beyond words must always spring
from everyday life, for everyday life is the
raw material of prayer.

PRAYER BEFORE
A TWENTY-DOLLAR BILL

We can hardly respect money enough for the blood and toil it represents.

Money is frightening. It can serve or destroy man.

"Corruption has fallen on your riches; all the fine clothes are left moth-eaten, and the gold and silver have long lain rusting. That rust will bear witness against you. . . . You have kept back the pay of the workmen who reaped your lands, and it is there to cry out against you; the Lord of hosts has listened to their complaint." (James V, 2, 4, KV)

"Sell what you have, and give alms, so providing yourselves with a purse that time cannot wear holes in, an inexhaustible treasure laid up in heaven, where no thief comes near, no moth consumes. Where your treasure-house is, there your heart is too." (Luke XII, 33-34, KV)

31

Lord, see this bill! It frightens me.
You know its secrets, you know its history.
How heavy it is!
It scares me, for it cannot speak.
It will never tell all it hides in its creases.
It will never reveal all the struggles and efforts it represents, all
    the disillusionment and slighted dignity.
It is stained with sweat and blood,
It is laden with all the weight of the human toil which makes
    its worth.

It is heavy, heavy, Lord.
It fills me with awe, it frightens me.
For it has death on its conscience . . .
All the poor fellows who killed themselves for it,
To possess it for a few hours,
To have through it a little pleasure, a little joy, a little life.

Through how many hands has it passed Lord?
And what has it done in the course of its long, silent journeys?

It has offered white roses to the radiant fiancée.
It has paid for the baptismal party, and fed the rosy-cheeked baby.
It has provided bread for the family table.
Because of it there was laughing among the young and joy among
    the elders.
It has paid for the saving visit of the doctor,
It has bought the book that taught the youngster,
It has clothed the young girl.

But it has sent the letter breaking the engagement,
It has paid for the death of the baby in its mother's womb,
It has bought the liquor that made the drunkard,
It has produced the movie unfit for children,
And has recorded the indecent song.
It has broken the morals of the adolescent and made of the adult
   a thief.
It has bought for a few hours the body of a woman.
It has paid for the weapons of the crime and for the wood of
   the coffin.

O Lord, I offer you this bill with its joyous mysteries, its sorrowful mysteries.
I thank you for all the life and joy it has given.
I ask your forgiveness for the harm it has done.
But above all, Lord, I offer it to you as a symbol of all the labors
   of men, indestructible money, which tomorrow will be
   changed into your eternal life.

THE PORNOGRAPHIC MAGAZINE

The body is matter, but it is God's creation, and spirit ennobles it. The body of a Christian who is conscious of God's life in him becomes the temple of the Holy Spirit and a member of Christ. Hence its dignity. When it is neglected or scoffed at, God himself is insulted.

"Surely you know that you are God's temple, where the Spirit of God dwells. Anyone who destroys God's temple will himself be destroyed by God, because the temple of God is holy; and that temple you are." (I Corinthians III, 16-17)

"Anyone who loves me will heed what I say; then my Father will love him, and we will come to him and make our dwelling with him. . . ." (John XIV, 23)

"Now you are Christ's body, and each of you a limb or organ of it." (I Corinthians XII, 27)

*"I will unfold a mystery: . . . we shall all be changed in a flash,
. . . and the dead will rise immortal. . . ."* (I Corinthians XV, 51-52)

"So the Word became flesh. . . ." (John I, 14)

Lord, I am ashamed of this magazine.
You must be profoundly hurt in your infinite purity.

The office employees all contributed to buy it.
The boy ran to fetch it,
And pored over it on the way back.
Here it is.
On its shining pages, naked bodies are exposed;
Going from office to office, from hand to hand—
Such foolish giggles, such lustful glances . . .
Empty bodies, soulless bodies,
Adult toys for the hardened and the soiled.

And yet, Lord, man's body *is* beautiful.
From the beginning you, the supreme artist, held the model
    before you, knowing that one day you would dwell in a
    human body when taking on the nature of man.
Slowly you shaped it with your powerful hands; and into its
    inert matter you breathed a living soul.
From then on, Lord, you asked us to respect the body, for the
    whole body is a conveyor of the spirit,
And we need this sensitive instrument that our spirits may com-
    mune with those of our brothers.

Words, in long processions, lead us toward other souls.
A smile on our lips, the expression in our eyes, reveal the soul.
The clasp of a hand carries our soul to a friend,
A kiss yields it to the loved one,
The embrace of the couple unites two souls in quest of a new
    child of God.

But it was not enough for you, Lord, to make of our flesh the
    visible sign of the spirit.
Through your grace the Christian's body became sacred, the
    temple of the Trinity.
A member of the Lord, and a bearer of his God,
Supreme dignity of this splendid body!

Here, Lord, before you, tonight, are the bodies of sleeping men:

The pure body of the tiny child,
The soiled body of the prostitute,
The vigorous body of the athlete,
The exhausted body of the factory worker,
The soft body of the playboy,
The surfeited body of the rich man,
The battered body of the poor man,
The beaten body of the slum child,
The feverish body of the sick man,
The painful body of the injured man,
The paralyzed body of the cripple,

all bodies, Lord, of all ages.

Here is the body of the fragile new-born baby, plucked like ripe fruit from its mother.
Here is the body of the light-hearted child who falls and gets up, unmindful of his cuts.
Here is the body of the worried adolescent who doesn't know that it's a fine thing to grow up.
Here is the body of the grown man, powerful and proud of his strength.
Here is the body of the old man, gradually failing.

I offer them all to you, Lord, and I ask you to bless them, while they lie in silence, wrapped in your night.
Left by their sleeping souls, they are there before your eyes, your own.
Tomorrow, shaken from their sleep, they will have to resume work.
May they be servants and not masters,
Welcoming homes and not prisons,
Temples of the living God, and not tombs.
May these bodies be developed, purified, transfigured by those who dwell in them,
And may we find them, at the end of their days, faithful companions, illumined by the beauty of their souls,

In your sight, Lord, and in your mother's,
Since you both belong to our earth,
And all the bodies of men will be the guests in glory of your eternal heaven.

THE TRACTOR

Machines are a means of progress if, by greatly increasing man's strength, they serve him. Unfortunately, too often man is a slave to their rhythmic beat and power. Machines are the servants of profit, but man is the servant of machines. We must struggle to re-establish a balance. As man extends himself and becomes more powerful through machines, he should also develop his spirit. He must rise above his mechanical work, master it and offer it to God.

"Whatever you are doing, whether you speak or act, do everything in the name of the Lord Jesus, giving thanks to God the Father through him." (Colossians III, 17)

I don't like tractors, Lord.
I saw one in a field a while ago,
And I loathed it.

Tractors are conceited.
They crush man with all their strength.
They never look at him, they just move forward.
But when they move forward, they crawl, and *that* pleases me.

They are ugly,
They move clumsily, shaking their heavy shells,
Their silly noses upturned, panting,
Coughing their deep, measured, mechanical cough.
But they are stronger than man, Lord.
Regularly, imperturbably, they pull their load;
They pull what a thousand human arms could not move,
They carry what a thousand human hands could not lift.
A tractor is ugly, yet it is strong and I need it.
But it needs me, it needs man.
It needs man to exist; it is man who made it.
It needs man to move; it is man who starts it going.
It needs man to go forward; it is man who steers it.
It needs man, especially, that it may be offered up,
For a tractor has no soul, Lord, and it is man who must lend
　　it his own.

I offer you tonight, Lord, the work of all the tractors in the
　　country, of all the tractors in the world.
I offer you the efforts of all the machines that have no soul with
　　which to offer themselves.
I pray that they may not crush man with their haughty power,
　　but rather that they shall serve him;
I pray that man, in the freedom of his soul, shall dominate
　　them,
And thus praise you by their work, glorify you,
And share in creation's Solemn Mass which is said every day
　　through human labor, and will be said until the end of
　　time.

THE FUNERAL

For a Christian, death does not exist, or, rather, it is only a starting-point and not an end. The Church sings at Masses for the Dead: "Life is not taken away, it is changed." The anniversary of the death of the blessed it calls a "birthday." Saint Thérèse of Lisieux, on her deathbed, murmured, "I am not dying, I am entering into life."

Our dead are alive, and, unless they are condemned forever, we can find them again in God. If we wish to live eternally with them, we must meet with Christ, listen to him and commune with him.

"I am the resurrection and I am life." (John XI, 25)

"In very truth I tell you, if anyone obeys my teaching he shall never know what it is to die." (John VIII, 51)

"I am that living bread . . . if anyone eats this bread he shall live forever." (John VI, 51)

"Now if this is what we proclaim, that Christ was raised from the dead, how can some of you say there is no resurrection of the dead? . . . if Christ was not raised, then our gospel is null and void, and so is your faith. . . . If it is for this life only that Christ has given us hope, we of all men are most to be pitied."
(I Corinthians XV, 12, 14, 19)

People were following:
The family—some crying,
Some pretending to cry;
Friends—some grieving,
Some bored or chatting.

Leaving the cemetery, some of the family were sobbing: All is
     finished.
Others were sniffling: "Come, come, my dear, courage: it's
     finished!"
Some friends murmured: "Poor man, that's how we'll all finish."
And others sighed in relief: "Well, it's finished."

And I was thinking that everything was just beginning.

Yes, he had finished the last rehearsal, but the play was just
     beginning.
The years of training were over, but the eternal work was about
     to start.
He had just been born to life,
The real life,

41

Life that's going to last,
Life eternal.

As if there were dead people!
There are no dead people, Lord.
There are only the living, on earth and beyond.
Death exists, Lord,
But it's nothing but a moment,
A second, a step,
The step from provisional to permanent,
From temporal to eternal.
As in the death of the child the adolescent is born,
        from the caterpillar emerges the butterfly,
        from the grain the full-blown sheath.

Death, grotesque character, bogey-man of little children, non-
        existent phantom,
I don't take you seriously,
But I am disgusted with you.
You terrify the world,
You frighten and deceive men,
And yet your only reason for existing is Life, and you are not
        able to take from us those that we love.

But where are they, Lord, those that I have loved?
Are they in ecstasy, taken up with holy loving in harmony with
        the Trinity?
Are they tormented in the night, burning with desire to love
        with an infinite love?
Are they in despair, condemned to their own selves because they
        preferred themselves to others? Consumed with hate be-
        cause they can no longer love?

42

Lord, my loved ones are near me,
I know that they live in the spirit.
My eyes can't see them because they have left their bodies for a
    moment, as one steps out of one's clothing.
Their souls, deprived of their bodily vesture, no longer com-
    municate with me.

But in you, Lord, I hear them calling me,
I see them beckoning to me,
I hear them giving me advice,
For they are now more vividly present.
Before, our bodies touched, but not our souls.
Now I meet them when I meet you.
I receive them when I receive you.
I love them when I love you.
Oh, my loved ones, eternally alive, who live in me,
Help me to learn thoroughly in this short life how to live
    eternally.

Lord, I love you, and I want to love you more.
It's you who make love eternal, and I want to love eternally.

THE SEA

Lives that are effective are not always those that attract attention. They are never those of the proud who storm against obstacles which cannot be removed. Lives lived humbly, under the eyes of God, illumined by his grace and radiant with love for others, are always effective.

"Love is patient; love is kind and envies no one. Love is never boastful, nor conceited, nor rude; never selfish, not quick to take offence. Love keeps no score of wrongs; does not gloat over other men's sins, but delights in the truth. There is nothing love cannot face; there is no limit to its faith, its hope, and its endurance."
(I Corinthians XIII, 4-7)

Lord, I saw the sea attacking the rocks, somber and raging.
From afar the waves gained momentum.
High and proud they leaped, jostling one another to be the first
    to strike.
When the white foam drew back, leaving the rock clear, they
    gathered themselves to rush forward again.

44

The other day I saw the sea calm and serene.

The waves came from afar, creeping, not to draw attention;

Quietly holding hands, they slipped noiselessly and stretched at full length on the sand, to touch the shore with the tips of their beautiful, mossy fingers.

The sun gently caressed them, and they generously returned streams of light.

Lord, grant that I may avoid useless attacks that tire and wound without achieving results.

Keep me from these angry outbursts that draw attention but leave one uselessly weakened.

Keep me from wanting always, in my conceit, to outstrip others, crushing those in my way.

Wipe from my face the sullen, subduing look.

Rather, Lord, grant that I may live my days calmly and fully, as the sea slowly covers the whole shore.

Make me humble like her, as, silently and gently, she spreads out, unnoticed.

May I wait for my brothers and match my pace to theirs, that I may move upward with them.

Grant me the triumphant perseverance of the waters.

May each of my retreats turn into an advance.

Give my face the light of clear waters;

Give my soul the whiteness of foam.

Illumine my life, that it may sing like sunbeams on the surface of the sea.

But above all, Lord, may I not keep this Light for myself, and may all those who come near me return home eager to bathe in your eternal grace.

EYES*

Man's eyes have great power, for they convey the soul. When God dwells in a man, his eyes can carry God to men.

"As he was starting out on a journey, a stranger ran up, and, kneeling before him, asked, 'Good Master, what must I do to win eternal life?' Jesus said to him, '. . . You know the command- ment: Do not murder; . . .' 'But, Master,' he replied, 'I have kept all these since I was a boy.' Jesus looked straight at him; his heart warmed to him, and he said, 'One thing you lack: go, sell everything you have . . . and come, follow me.'" (Mark X, 17-21)

"A serving-maid who saw him sitting in the firelight stared at him and said, 'This man was with him too.' But he denied it: 'Woman,' he said, 'I do not know him'. . . . At that moment, while he was still speaking, a cock crew; and the Lord turned and looked straight at Peter. And Peter remembered the Lord's words. . . . He went outside, and wept bitterly." (Luke XXII, 56-57, 60-62)

* *Le Regard.* This word has no exact English equivalent.

"When he came in sight of the city, he wept over it and said, 'If only you had known, on this great day, the way that leads to peace.' " (John I, 41-42)

"[Andrew] brought Simon to Jesus, who looked him in the face, and said, 'You are Simon, son of John. You shall be called Cephas.' " (John I, 42)

"The lamp of the body is the eye. If your eyes are sound, you will have light for your whole body; if the eyes are bad, your whole body will be in darkness." (Matthew VI, 22)

I am now about to close my eyelids, Lord,
For my eyes this evening have finished their work,
And my vagrant glances will return home,
Having strolled for a day in the market place.

Thank you, Lord, for my eyes, windows open on the wide world;
Thank you for their look that carries my soul as the broad sun-
    beam carries the light and warmth of your sun.
I pray to you, during the night, that tomorrow, when I open my
    eyes to the clear morning,
They shall be ready to serve both my soul and my God.

May my eyes be clear and straightforward, Lord, and give others
    a hunger for purity;

May my look never be one of disappointment,
                              disillusionment,
                              despair,

But may it know how to admire,
                    contemplate,
                    adore.

May my eyes learn to close in order to find you more easily;
But may they never turn away from the world because they are
    afraid.
May my eyes be penetrating enough to recognize your Presence
    in the world,
And may they never shut on the afflictions of men.

May my eyes be firm and steady,
But may they also know how to soften in pity and be capable
    of tears.

May my gaze not soil the one it touches,
May it not disturb, but may it bring peace.
May it not sadden, but rather may it transmit joy.
May it not attract in order to hold captive,
But rather may it persuade others to rise above themselves
    to you.

May my eyes disquiet the sinner because in them he will see
    your light,
But may their reproach lead to encouragement.

Grant that my eyes may be startling because they are an
    encounter, an encounter with God.
Grant that they be a call,
    a loud clear call
    that brings all the world to its doorstep,
Not because of me, Lord,
But because you are to pass by.

That my eyes may be all this, Lord,
Once more, this evening,
I give you my soul,
I give you my body,
I give you my eyes,
That when they look at men, my brothers,
It may be you who look at them
And you who beckon.

TO LOVE:
THE PRAYER OF THE ADOLESCENT

Adolescence is not the "silly age"; it is the splendid age, the age
when God, through the laws of nature, puts in the young person's
body and heart a deep call towards a body other than his own,
towards a heart other than his own.

May every young person then have someone to explain this
to him; parents who love him enough not to cling to him
selfishly, but to direct his attention to the new and clear road
along which "she" will appear.

May he have a friend, a brother, who will help him to forget
himself for others, lest he become a slave to himself, incapable
of loving.

*"We for our part have crossed over from death to life; this we
know, because we love our brothers. The man who does not love
is still in the realm of death, ... It is by this that we know
what love is: that Christ laid down his life for us. And we in our
turn are bound to lay down our lives for our brothers."* (I John
III, 14, 16)

*"Dear friends, let us love one another, because love is from
God . . . but the unloving know nothing of God. For God is love."*
(I John IV, 7-8)

I want to love, Lord,
I need to love.
All my being is desire;
My heart,
My body,
    yearn in the night towards an unknown one to love.
My arms thrash about, and I can seize on no object for my love.
I am alone and want to be two.
I speak, and no one is there to listen.
I live, and no one is there to share my life.
Why be so rich and have no one to enrich?
Where does this love come from?
Where is it going?
I want to love, Lord,
I need to love.

Here this evening, Lord, is all my love, unused.

Listen, son,
Stop,
    and make, silently, a long pilgrimage to the bottom of
    your heart.
Walk by the side of your love so new, as one follows a brook
    to find its source,
And at the very end, deep within you, in the infinite mystery
    of your troubled soul, you will meet me.
For I call myself Love, son,

52

And from the beginning I have been nothing but Love,
And Love is in you.

It is I who made you to love,
To love eternally;
And your love will pass through another self of yours—
It is she that you seek;
Set your mind at rest; she is on your way,
      on the way since the beginning,
      the way of my love.
  ou must wait for her coming.
She is approaching,
You are approaching.
You will recognize each other,
For I've made her body for you, I've made yours for her.
I've made your heart for her, I've made hers for you,
And you seek each other, in the night,
In "my night," which will become Light if you trust me.

Keep yourself for her, son,
As she is keeping herself for you.
I shall keep you for one another,
And, since you hunger for love, I've put on your way all your
      brothers to love.
Believe me, it's a long apprenticeship, learning to love,
And there are not several kinds of love:
Loving is always leaving oneself to go towards others. . . .

Lord, help me to forget myself for others, my brothers,
That in giving myself I may teach myself to love.

I FOUND MARCEL ALONE

It is not easy to love, and if, all too often, our loves miscarry, isn't it because of a dreadful mistake? Were not our loves simply "the clash of two egoisms"? Did we even succeed in crossing the threshold of our selves? If true love gives joy, it is bought by suffering.

". . . they are no longer two individuals: they are one flesh. What God has joined together, man must not separate." (Mark X, 8-9)

". . . men also are bound to love their wives, as they love their own bodies. In loving his wife a man loves himself. For no one ever hated his own body: on the contrary, he provides and cares for it; and that is how Christ treats the Church, because it is his body, of which we are living parts. Thus it is that (in the words of Scripture) 'a man shall leave his father and mother and shall be joined to his wife, and the two shall become a single body.' It is a great truth that is hidden here. I for my part prefer it to Christ and to the church, . . . each of you must love his wife as his very self; and the woman must see to it that she pays her husband all respect." (Ephesians V, 28-33)

It was about noon when I knocked at his door.
I found Marcel alone, still lying on the bed which was now too
   big for him;
His wife had left him a few days ago.

It hurt me, Lord, to see that poor fellow so discouraged, that
   house half-empty.
A presence was lacking,
A love was lacking.
I missed the bunch of flowers on the mantelpiece, the powder
   and lipstick on the wash-basin, the bureau scarf on the
   bureau and the chairs properly arranged.
I found the sheets dirty on a bed wrinkled like an old face, the
   ash-trays filled to overflowing, shoes scattered on the floor,
   a rag on the easy-chair, and the blinds closed.
It was dark, dismal, and stuffy.

It hurt me, Lord.
I felt something torn,
   something unbalanced,
Like a mechanism gone wrong,
Like a man with broken bones.

And I reflected that what you had planned was good,
And that there can be no order and beauty, love and joy, outside
   of your plan.

I pray to you tonight, Lord,
    for Marcel and for her
    and for the other one
    and for the wife of the other one
    and for his children
    and for the families involved
    and for the neighbors who gossip
    and for the colleagues who judge.

I ask of you forgiveness
    for all these lacerations,
    for all these wounds,
    and for your blood poured out, because of these wounds,
    in your Mystical Body.
I pray to you tonight, Lord, for myself and for all my friends.
Teach us to love.

It is not easy to love, son.
Often when you think you love, it is only yourself that you love,
    and you spoil everything, you shatter everything.

To love is to meet oneself, and to meet oneself one must be
    willing to leave oneself and go towards another.
To love is to commune, and to commune one must forget oneself
    for another,
One must die to self completely for another.
To love hurts, you know, son,
For since the Fall—listen carefully, son—to love is to crucify
    self for another.

56

THE DELINQUENT

Man is alone since he is unique, but he is made for communion. Sin divides and isolates us. We must grow closer, share the burden of each other's sins—and atone for them—to overcome the obstacle to our oneness. Solitude causes suffering; it is not part of the Father's plan. Redemptive love alone can conquer it and cement our unity.

"A man was on his way from Jerusalem down to Jericho when he fell in with robbers, who stripped him, beat him, and went off leaving him half dead. It so happened that a priest was going down by the same road; but when he saw him, he went past on the other side. So too a Levite came to the place, and when he saw him went past on the other side. But a Samaritan who was making the journey came upon him, and when he saw him was moved to pity. He went up and bandaged his wounds, bathing them with oil and wine. Then he lifted him on to his own beast, brought him to an inn, and looked after him there. Next day he produced two silver pieces and gave them to the innkeeper, and said, 'Look after him; and if you spend any more, I will repay you on my way back.'" (Luke X, 30-35)

I know his secret,
His weighty secret.
How, Lord, can it be carried by this big boy with the childish
face grown old too soon?

I wanted him to tell it to me,
To give it to me to bear with him.
For long months now I have been stretching my hand towards
this young, crushed brother.
Eagerly he seizes that hand, caresses it, kisses it . . . but over the
gulf that separates us.
When I want gently to draw him closer, he backs away, for in
his other hand he carries his secret, too heavy for him to
hand to me.
Lord, he hurts me.
I look at him from a distance, and cannot get near him,
He looks at me and cannot come closer.

We both suffer.
He suffers the more, and I can hardly bear it, for my love is too
limited, Lord; each time that I try to span his solitude, my
bridge is too short and does not touch his shore.
And I see him, on the edge of his suffering, hesitating, getting set,
but drawing back again in desperation, for the distance is
too great and the burden is too heavy.
Yesterday, Lord, he leaned towards me, said a word—then took
it back; his whole body quivered with the weight of the
secret which approached his lips but rolled back again to
the depths of his solitude.
He did not cry, but I wiped off the drops of perspiration beading
his forehead.
I cannot take his burden from him; he must give it to me.
I see it, and I cannot grasp it.

58

You do not want me to take it, Lord, since he does not want that.
I have no right to violate his suffering.

I am thinking tonight, Lord, of all the isolated ones,
Of all those who are alone, terribly alone,
Because they have never let go and been carried by anyone,
Because they have never given themselves to you, Lord.
Those who know something that others will never know;
Those who suffer from a sore that no one can ever tend,
Those who bleed from a wound that no one will ever heal;
Those who are scarred by a terrible blow that no one will ever
    suspect;
Those who have, locked in the terrifying silence of their hearts, a
    harvest of humiliations, despairs, hatreds,
Those who have hidden a mortal sin—cold sepulchres behind
    cheerful façades.

The solitude of man frightens me, Lord;
Every man is alone, since he is unique,
And that solitude is sacred; he alone can break through it, con-
    fide and share confidences.
He alone can pass from solitude to communion.
And you want this communion, Lord. You want us to be united
    with one another,
In spite of the deep gulf that we have dug between us by sin,
You want us to be united as your Father and you are united.

Lord, that boy hurts me, as do all isolated ones;
Grant that I may love them enough to break through their
    isolation.
Grant that I may pass through the world with all doors open,
My house entirely empty, available, welcoming.

Help me to withdraw so as to embarrass no one,
That others may come in without asking,
That they may deposit their burdens without being seen.
And I'll come, silently, to get them by night
And you, Lord, will help me to bear them.

THANK YOU

We must know how to say, "Thank You." Our days are filled with the gifts the Lord showers on us. If we were in the habit of taking stock of them, at night we should be like a "queen for a day," dazzled and happy with so many blessings. We should then be grateful to God, secure because he gives us everything, joyful because we know that every day he will renew his gifts.

Everything is a gift from God, even the smallest things, and it's the sum of these gifts that makes a life beautiful or sad, depending on how we use them.

"All good giving and every perfect gift comes from above, from the Father of the lights of heaven. With him there is no variation, no play of passing shadows." (James I, 17)

Thank you, Lord, thank you.
Thank you for all the gifts that you have given me today,
Thank you for all I have seen, heard, received.

61

Thank you for the water that woke me up, the soap that smells good, the toothpaste that refreshes.

Thank you for the clothes that protect me, for their color and their cut.

Thank you for the newspaper so faithfully there, for the comics (my morning smile), for the report of useful meetings, for justice done and for big games won.

Thank you for the street-cleaning truck and the men who run it, for their morning shouts and all the early noises.

Thank you for my work, my tools, my efforts.

Thank you for the metal in my hands, for the whine of the steel biting into it, for the satisfied look of the supervisor and the load of finished pieces.

Thank you for Jim who lent me his file, for Danny who gave me a cigarette, for Charlie who held the door for me.

Thank you for the welcoming street that led me there, for the shop windows, for the cars, for the passers-by, for all the life that flowed swiftly between the windowed walls of the houses.

Thank you for the food that sustained me, for the glass of beer that refreshed me.

Thank you for the car that meekly took me where I wanted to be, for the gas that made it go, for the wind that caressed my face and for the trees that nodded to me on the way.

Thank you for the boy I watched playing on the sidewalk opposite,

Thank you for his roller-skates and for his comical face when he fell.

62

Thank you for the morning greetings I received, and for all the smiles.

Thank you for the mother who welcomes me at home, for her tactful affection, for her silent presence.

Thank you for the roof that shelters me, for the lamp that lights me, for the radio that plays, for the news, for music and singing.

Thank you for the bunch of flowers, so pretty on my table.

Thank you for the tranquil night.
Thank you for the stars.
Thank you for the silence.

Thank you for the time you have given me.
Thank you for life.
Thank you for grace.

Thank you for being there, Lord.
Thank you for listening to me, for taking me seriously, for gathering my gifts in your hands to offer them to your Father.
Thank you, Lord,
Thank you.

THE PRIEST:
A PRAYER ON SUNDAY NIGHT

People ask a great deal of their priest, and they should. But they should also understand that it is not easy to be a priest. He has given himself in all the ardor of youth, yet he still remains a man, and every day the man in him tries to take back what he has surrendered. It is a continual struggle to remain completely at the service of Christ and of others.

A priest needs no praise or embarrassing gifts; what he needs is that those committed to his charge should, by loving their fellows more and more, prove to him that he has not given his life in vain. And as he remains a man, he may need, once in a while, a delicate gesture of disinterested friendship . . . some Sunday night when he is alone.

"Come with me, and I will make you fishers of men." (Mark I, 17) .

"You did not choose me: I chose you. I appointed you to go on and bear fruit that shall last. . . ." (John XV, 16)

64

"Forgetting what is behind me, and reaching out for that which lies ahead, I press towards the goal to win the prize which is God's call to the life above, in Christ Jesus." (Philippians III, 13-14)

Tonight, Lord, I am alone.
Little by little the sounds died down in the church,
The people went away,
And I came home,
Alone.

I passed people who were returning from a walk.
I went by the movie house that was disgorging its crowd.
I skirted café terraces where tired strollers were trying to prolong
    the pleasure of a Sunday holiday.
I bumped into youngsters playing on the sidewalk,
Youngsters, Lord,
Other people's youngsters, who will never be my own.

Here I am, Lord,
Alone.
The silence troubles me,
The solitude oppresses me.

. . . .

Lord, I'm thirty-five years old,
A body made like others,
Arms ready for work,

A heart meant for love,
But I've given you all.
It's true, of course, that you needed it.
I've given you all, but it's hard, Lord.
It's hard to give one's body; it would like to give itself to others.
It's hard to love everyone and to claim no one.
It's hard to shake a hand and not want to retain it.
It's hard to inspire affection, only to give it to you.
It's hard to be nothing to oneself in order to be everything to
    others.
It's hard to be like others, among others, and to be other.
It's hard always to give without trying to receive.
It's hard to seek out others and to be, oneself, unsought.
It's hard to suffer from the sins of others, and yet be obliged to
    hear and bear them.
It's hard to be told secrets, and be unable to share them.
It's hard to carry others and never, even for a moment, be
    carried.
It's hard to sustain the feeble and never be able to lean on one
    who is strong.
It's hard to be alone,
Alone before everyone,
Alone before the world,
Alone before suffering,
    death,
    sin.

Son, you are not alone,
I am with you;
I am you.

For I needed another human instrument to continue my Incarnation and my Redemption.
Out of all eternity, I chose you,
I need you.

I need your hands to continue to bless,
I need your lips to continue to speak,
I need your body to continue to suffer,
I need your heart to continue to love,
I need you to continue to save.
Stay with me, son.

Here I am, Lord;
Here is my body,
Here is my heart,
Here is my soul.
Grant that I may be big enough to reach the world,
Strong enough to carry it,
Pure enough to embrace it without wanting to keep it.
Grant that I may be a meeting-place, but a temporary one,
A road that does not end in itself, because everything to be gathered there, everything human, leads toward you.

Lord, tonight, while all is still and I feel sharply the sting of solitude,
While men devour my soul and I feel incapable of satisfying their hunger,
While the whole world presses on my shoulders with all its weight of misery and sin,

I repeat to you my "yes"—not in a burst of laughter, but slowly,
   clearly, humbly,
Alone, Lord, before you,
In the peace of the evening.

I SPOKE, LORD

Speech is God's gift. We shall have to account for it. It is through words that we communicate with each other and that we reveal what we are. We haven't the right to be silent, but speaking is a serious matter, and we must weigh our words in the sight of God.

"I tell you this: there is not a thoughtless word that comes from men's lips but they will have to account for it on the day of judgment. For out of your own mouth you will be acquitted; out of your own mouth you will be condemned." (Matthew XII, 36-37)

"Not everyone who calls me 'Lord, Lord' will enter the kingdom of Heaven, but only those who do the will of my heavenly Father. When that day comes, many will say to me, 'Lord, Lord, did we not phophesy in your name, cast out devils in your name, and in your name perform many miracles?' Then I will tell them to their face, 'I never knew you: out of my sight, you and your wicked ways!'" (Matthew VII, 21-23)

I spoke, Lord, and I am furious.

I am furious because I worked so hard with gestures and with
words.

I threw my whole self into them, and I'm afraid the essential
didn't get across.

For the essential is not mine, and words alone are too shallow to
hold it.

I spoke, Lord, and I am worried.

I am afraid of speaking, for speaking is serious;

It's serious to disturb others, to bring them out, to keep them on
their doorsteps;

It's serious to keep them waiting, with outstretched hands and
longing hearts, seeking for light or some courage to live
and act.

Suppose, Lord, that I should send them away, empty-handed!

And yet, I must speak.

You have given me speech for a few years, and I must make use
of it.

I owe my soul to others, and words are crowding to my lips to
bring it to them.

For the soul could hardly express itself if speech were taken
from it.

We know nothing of the infant inside its little body,

And the whole family rejoices when, word by word, phrase by
phrase, its soul is revealed to them.

But when one of the family is dying, the others stand despairing
by his bed, listening intently to his last words.

He passes on, locked in silence, and his relatives will no longer
know his soul, once they have shut his eyes and closed his
lips.

Speech, Lord, is a gift, and I have no right to be quiet through
   pride, cowardice, negligence or apathy.
Others have a right to my words, to my soul,
For I have a message from you to give them,
And none other than I, Lord, can give it to them.
I have something to say—short perhaps, but welling up from my
   life—from which I cannot turn.
But my words must be true words.
It would be a breach of trust to seek the attention of another,
   and under the cover of words not to reveal the truth of the
   soul.
The words that I pour out must be living words, full of the
   mysteries that my unique soul has grasped, mysteries of the
   world and of man.
The words that I speak must be conveyors of God, for the lips
   that you have given me, Lord, are made to reveal my soul,
   and my soul knows you and holds you close.

Forgive me, Lord, for having spoken so badly,
Forgive me for having spoken often to no purpose;
Forgive me for the days when I tarnished my lips with hollow
   words,
      false words,
      cowardly words,
   words through which you could not pass.
Uphold me when I must speak in a meeting, intervene in a dis-
   cussion, talk with a brother.
Grant above all, Lord, that my words may be like the sowing of
   seeds,
And that those who hear them may look to a fine harvest.

71

THAT FACE, LORD, HAUNTS ME

If, where the Father has placed us, we do not fight with all our strength against the world in disorder, we are not real Christians. We do not love God. For he said it through St. John: "If he does not love the brother whom he has seen, it cannot be that he loves God whom he has not seen" (I John IV, 20); and, "My children, love must not be a matter of words or talk; it must be genuine, and show itself in action" (I John III, 18).

But it isn't simply by improving the look of a man's face that a Christian can bring peace to his conscience; it is by finding and tackling all the social and moral disorders which have produced that face.

The poor will judge us.

"And they too will reply, 'Lord, when was it that we saw you hungry or thirsty or a stranger or naked or ill or in prison, and did nothing for you?' And he will answer, 'I tell you this: anything you did not do for one of these, however humble, you did not do for me.'" (Matthew XXV, 44-45)

That face, Lord, has haunted me all evening.
It is a living reproach,
A prolonged cry that reaches me even in my quietude.

That face is young, Lord, yet man's sins have attacked it;
He was defenseless and exposed to their blows.

They came from all over;
Destitution came,
The shanty,
The dilapidated bed,
The foul air,
Smoke,
Alcohol,
Hunger,
The hospital,
The sanatorium.

Work—crushing, humiliating.
Unemployment,
The Depression,
War.

Frenzied dances,
Revolting songs,
Demoralizing movies,
Languorous music,
Unclean and deceitful kisses.

The struggle to live,
Rebellion,
Brawls,
Cries,
Blows,
Hate.

They came from all over;
Men with their horrid selfishness, their dreadful faces,
    their big dirty fingers,
    their broken nails,
    their fetid breath.
They hastened here from the ends of the earth, from the
    bounds of time.
And slowly, one after another,
Or suddenly, all together, like brutes,
They struck,
    whipped,
    lashed,
    wrought,
    moulded,
    hammered,
    engraved,
    sculptured.

And here at last is this face, this poor face;
It took eighteen years to fashion it,
It took hundreds of centuries to produce it.
Ecce Homo: behold the man.

Here is this poor face of a man, like an open book,
The book of the miseries and sins of men;

74

the book of selfishness,
           conceit,
           cowardice;
the book of greed,
           lust,
           abdications,
           compromises.

Here it is like a mournful protest,
      like a cry of revolt,
      but also like a heart-rending call,
For behind this ridiculous, grimacing face,
Behind those uneasy eyes—
Like the clasped hands of one drowned, white on the dark sur-
      face of the pool—
Is a light,
A flame,
A tragic supplication,
The infinite desire of a soul to live above its mire.

Lord, that face haunts me, it frightens me, it condemns me;
For, with everyone else, I have made it, or allowed it to be made.
And I realize, Lord, that this boy is my brother, and yours.

What have we done with a member of your family!

I fear your judgment, Lord.
It seems to me that at the end of time all the faces of brothers,
      and especially those of my town, my neighborhood, my
      work, will be lined up before me,
And in your merciless light I shall recognize in these faces

the lines that I have cut,
the mouth that I have twisted,
the eyes that I have darkened,
and those whose light I have extinguished.

They will come, those that I have known and those that I have
not known, those of my time and all those that have followed, fashioned by the workshop of the world.

And I shall stand still, terrified, silent.
It is then, O Lord, that you will say to me

   ... "It was I. ..."

. . . .
Lord, forgive me for that face which has condemned me,
Lord, thank you for that face which has awakened me.

HUNGER

All men are our brothers, for the blood of Christ made us sons of the same Father. When a member of a family suffers and dies, the other members grieve. Since we know now that millions of men die of hunger every year, we can no longer live as before. Even if my means permit it, a mode of living beyond that which is fitting and necessary is a sin. We repeat: it is a sin to live without fighting with all our might, where we are, for more justice in the world.

"There was once a rich man, who dressed in purple and the finest linen, and feasted in great magnificence every day. At his gate, covered with sores, lay a poor man named Lazarus, who would have been glad to satisfy his hunger with the scraps from the rich man's table. Even the dogs used to come and lick his sores." (Luke XVI, 19-21)

"He said to his disciples, 'Make them sit down. . . .' Then, taking the five loaves and the two fishes, he looked up to heaven, said the blessing over them, broke them, and gave them to the disciples to distribute to the people. They all ate to their hearts' content." (Luke IX, 14-17)

☆

I have eaten,
I have eaten too much,
I have eaten because others did,
Because I was invited,
Because I was in the world and the world would not have under-
     stood;
And each dish,
Each mouthful,
Each swallow was hard to get down.
I have eaten too much, Lord,
While at that moment, in my town, more than fifteen hundred
     persons queued up at the breadline,
While in her attic a woman ate what she had salvaged that
     morning from the garbage cans.
While urchins in their tenement divided some scraps from the
     old folks' home,
While ten, a hundred, a thousand unfortunates throughout the
     world at that very moment twisted in pain and died of
     hunger before their despairing families.

Lord, it's terrible, for I know,
Men know, now.
They know that not only a few destitute are hungry, but hun-
     dreds at their own doors.
They know that not only several hundreds, but thousands are
     hungry on the borders of their country.
They know that not only thousands, but millions are hungry
     throughout the world.
Men have made a map of the geography of hunger,
Areas of starvation and death, appalling.
The figures stand out in stark and implacable truth.

78

Our minimum wage here for a month is, for millions and millions of human beings, their maximum wage for a year.
One-third of humanity is underfed.
Several million die of hunger in India in the course of one famine alone.
On an average, the Indians live for barely twenty-six years.

Lord, you see this map, you read these figures,
Not like a calm statistician in his office,
But like the father of a large family bending over the head of each of his sons.

Lord, you have seen this map, you have read these figures since the beginning of time,
And you told the story, for me, of the rich man at table and the poor starved Lazarus;
And you spoke, for me, of the Last Judgment.

". . . I was hungry. . . ."

Lord, you are terrible!
It's you who queue up at the breadline,
It's you who eat the scraps of garbage,
It's you who are tortured by hunger and starve to death,
It's you who die alone in a corner at twenty-six,
While in another corner of the great hall of the world—with some members of our family—I eat, without being hungry, what is needed to save you.

". . . I was hungry . . ."

Remind me of that, Lord, if I stop for a moment giving myself.
I'll never be through giving bread to my brothers, for there are
    too many of them.
There will always be some who won't have had their share.
I'll never be through fighting to get bread for all my brothers.

Lord, it isn't easy to feed the world.
I would rather say my prayers regularly, properly;
I would rather abstain on Fridays,
I would rather visit my pauper,
I would rather give to fairs and orphanages;
But apparently that isn't enough.
It's nothing, if one day you can say to me: "I was hungry!"

Lord, I'm no longer hungry,
Lord, I don't want to be hungry again.
Lord, I want to eat only what I need to live, to serve you and to
    fight for my brothers.
For you are hungry, Lord,
You die of hunger, while I am surfeited.

80

HOUSING

In the world's large cities the problem of housing is appalling.
It's our first duty to realize it. Many of the comfortably-housed
have never even been through the slum quarters of their city.
We must speak out, for public opinion is a powerful weapon
and each of us helps to create it. There are many organizations
that need our active help, or, at the very least, our support. If
we love our brothers, we shall always find a way, wherever we
are, to do something for them.

*"Suppose a brother or a sister is in rags with not enough food
for the day, and one of you says, 'Good luck to you, keep yourselves warm, and have plenty to eat,' but does nothing to sup-
ply their bodily needs, what is the good of that?"* (James II,
15-16)

Lord, I can't sleep; I have gotten out of bed to pray.
It is night outside, and the wind blows and the rain falls,
And the lights of the city, signs of the living, pierce the darkness.

They bother me, Lord, these lights—why are you showing them to me?

They beckon to me, and now they hold me captive, while the woes of the city murmur their muffled lament.

And I cannot escape them, Lord; I know these sufferings too well.

I see them rising before me,

I hear them speaking to me,

I feel them striking me,

They were bothering me when I was trying to sleep.

I know that in one single room thirteen crowded people are breathing on one another.

I know a mother who hooks the table and the chairs to the ceiling to make room for mattresses.

I know that rats come out to eat the crusts, and bite the babies.

I know a father who gets up to stretch oilcloth above the rain-soaked bed of his four children.

I know a mother who stays up all night, since there is room for only one bed, and the two children are sick.

I know a drunken father who vomits on the child sleeping beside him.

I know a big boy who runs away alone into the night because he can't take it any more.

I know that some men fight for the women, as there are three couples in the same attic.

I know a wife who avoids her husband, as there is no room for another baby at home.

I know a child who is quietly dying, soon to join his four little brothers.

I know . . .

I know hundreds of others—yet I was going to sleep peacefully between my nice white sheets.

I wish I didn't know, Lord.

82

I wish it were not true.
I wish I could convince myself that I'm dreaming,
I wish someone could prove that I'm exaggerating,
I wish they'd show me that all these people have only themselves
to blame, that it's their fault they are so miserable.
I'd like to be reassured, Lord, but I can't be. It's too late.
I've seen too much,
I've listened too much,
I've counted too much, and, Lord, these ruthless figures have
robbed me forever of my innocent tranquility.

So much the better, son,
For I, your God, your Father, am cross with you.
I gave you the world at the beginning of time, and I want each
of my children to have a home worthy of their Father in
my vast kingdom.
I trusted you, and your selfishness has spoiled everything.
It's one of your most serious sins, shared by many of you.
Woe unto you if, through your fault, a single one of my children
dies in body or in spirit.
I tell you, I will give to those the finest lodgings in Paradise.
But the thoughtless, the negligent, the selfish, who, well-sheltered
on earth, have forgotten others—they have had their re-
ward.
There will be no room for them in my Kingdom.

Come, son, ask forgiveness for yourself and for others tonight.
And tomorrow, fight with all your strength, for it hurts your
Father to see that once more there is no room for his Son at
the inn.

THE HOSPITAL

Suffering is a mystery, and only faith can throw light on it. Pain is not directly willed by God. Men have rejected his plan; they have thrown man and the universe out of balance, and so suffering was born. But Christ came to straighten out the disorder. He made of useless suffering the very means of redemption.

"Surely he hath borne our griefs, and carried our sorrows: yet we did esteem him stricken, smitten of God, and afflicted. But he was wounded for our transgressions, he was bruised for our iniquities: the chastisement of our peace was upon him; and with his stripes we are healed." (Isaiah LIII, 4-5)

This afternoon I went to see a patient at the hospital.
From pavilion to pavilion I walked, through that city of suffering, sensing the tragedies hardly concealed by the brightly painted walls and the flower-bordered lawns.
I had to go through a ward; I walked on tiptoe, hunting for my patient.

84

My eyes passed quickly and discreetly over the sick, as one
     touches a wound delicately to avoid hurting.
I felt uncomfortable,
Like the non-initiated traveler lost in a mysterious temple,
Like a pagan in the nave of a church.
At the very end of the second ward I found my patient,
And once there, I could only stammer. I had nothing to say.

Lord, suffering disturbs me, oppresses me.
I don't understand why you allow it.
Why, Lord?
Why this innocent child who has been moaning for a week, hor-
     ribly burned?
This man who has been dying for three days and three nights,
     calling for his mother?
This woman with cancer who in one month seems ten years
     older?
This workman fallen from his scaffolding, a broken puppet less
     than twenty years old?
This stranger, poor isolated wreck, who is one great open sore?
This girl in a cast, lying on a board for more than thirty years?
Why, Lord?
I don't understand.
Why this suffering in the world
          that shocks,
               isolates,
               revolts,
               shatters?
Why this hideous suffering that strikes blindly without seeming
     cause,
Falling unjustly on the good, and sparing the evil;
Which seems to withdraw, conquered by science, but comes back
     in another form, more powerful and more subtle?
I don't understand.

Suffering is odious and frightens me.
Why these people, Lord, and not others?
Why these, and not me?

Son, it is not I, your God, who have willed suffering; it is men.
They have brought it into the world in bringing sin,
Because sin is disorder, and disorder hurts.
There is for every sin, somewhere in the world and in time, a
    corresponding suffering.
And the more sins there are, the more suffering.

But I came, and I took all your sufferings upon me, as I took
    all your sins,
I took them and suffered them before you.
I transformed them, I made of them a treasure.
They are still an evil, but an evil with a purpose,
For through your sufferings, I accomplish Redemption.

HE WAS IN THE MIDDLE
OF THE STREET

The world is in such a state of disorder that many men, to earn
their living, are forced to take part in work that destroys others,
physically or morally. Victims of economic systems that are sinful, some are obliged to lie and to steal.

All those concerned should suffer profoundly from that tragic
situation. They share the responsibility for the state of the
world, and must recognize the sins of their society and blame
themselves. But just as true contrition is found only when one
seeks to change one's life, so true suffering for the sins of the
social order is found only when one works to change systems that
are inhuman. This is an absolute duty from which there is no
dispensation for the Christian.

*"You are the light of the world; a city cannot be hidden if it
is built on a mountain-top. A lamp is not lighted to be put away
under a bushel measure; it is put on the lamp-stand, to give
light to all the people of the house; and your light must shine
so brightly before men. . . ."* (Matthew V, 14-16, KV)

He was in the middle of the street,
Staggering, and singing at the top of his lungs in the husky
  voice of a drunk
People turned round and stopped, amused.
A policeman came silently from behind,
Grabbed him brutally by the shoulder, and took him to the
  police station.
He was still singing,
And people laughing.

I did not laugh, Lord.
I thought of his wife, who would wait in vain for him that night.
I thought of all the other drunks of the town,
    those of the pubs and the bars,
    those of living-rooms and cocktail parties.
I thought of their homecoming, at night;
    of the frightened youngsters,
    the empty wallets,
    the blows,
    the cries,
    the tears,
I thought of the children who would be born of drunken em-
  braces.

Now you have spread your night over the city, Lord,
And while tragedies unfold,
The men who have justified alcohol,
    produced alcohol,
    sold alcohol,
That same night sleep in peace.

I think of all those men, and I pity them;
      they have produced and sold misery,
      they have produced and sold sin.
I think of all the others, the crowd of others who work
      to destroy and not to build,
      to stupefy and not to uplift,
      to debase and not to ennoble.
I think especially, Lord, of the many men who work for war,
      who, to feed a family, have to work to destroy others, who,
      to live, must manufacture death.
I don't ask you to keep them all from their work—that is not
      possible.
But, Lord, may they question it;
      may their sleep be uneasy,
      may they fight in this world of disorder,
      may they act as leaven,
      may they be redeemers.

By all the wounded in soul and body, victims of the work of
      their brothers,
By all the dead for whom thousands of men have conscientiously
      manufactured death,
By that drunk, grotesque clown in the middle of the street,
By the humiliation and tears of his wife,
By the fear and cries of his children,
Lord, have pity on me, too often slumbering.
Lord, have pity also on the miserable men who are completely
      asleep and who collaborate in a world where brothers kill
      each other to earn their bread.

THE BALD HEAD

We have been in God's thought from all Eternity, and in his creative love his attention never leaves us. We must see in our brothers God's idea of them, and respect it. We must be attentive to them even as God is attentive to us.

"In him [Christ] everything in heaven and on earth was created, not only things visible but also the invisible . . . the whole universe has been created through him and for him. And he exists before everything, and all things are held together in him." (Colossians I, 16-17)

"But not a hair of your head shall be lost." (Luke XXI, 18)

"Are not sparrows five for twopence? And yet not one of them is overlooked by God. More than that, even the hairs of your head have all been counted. Have no fear; you are worth more than any number of sparrows." (Luke XII, 6-7)

For an hour it was before my eyes,
During the whole lecture.
That was a fine dome, Lord,
Polished, shining, girdled with a horse-shoe of hair carefully
arranged and sternly held to the pattern prescribed.
The lecture bored me:
I had time to think,
And I thought, Lord, that you knew this dome well.
It hasn't been out of your sight for years, and every day you say
"yes" when old Mother Nature asks permission to take a
few hairs more from the rapidly clearing field.
You said it in your Gospel: "not one hair of your head falls
without my permission."

It's true, Lord, that you are always thinking of us.
It's true, from the beginning of time, before we existed,
Even before the world existed,
You have been dreaming of me,
Thinking of me,
Loving me.
And it's true that your Love created me,
Not on an assembly-line, but unique,
The first one so made, and the last,
Indispensable to humanity.
It's true, Lord, that you have conceived for my life a unique
destiny.
It's true that you have an eternal plan for me alone,
A wonderful plan that you have always cherished in your heart,
as a father thinks over the smallest details in the life of his
little one still unborn.
It's true that, always bending over me, you guide me to bring
your plan about, light on my path and strength for my soul.
It's true that you are saddened when I stray or run away, but
that you hasten to pick me up if I stumble or fall.

Lord, you who make bald heads, but above all beautiful lives,
You, the divine Attentive One,
  the divine Patient One,
  the divine Present One,
See that at no time I forget your presence.
I don't ask you to bless what I myself have decided to do, but
Give me the grace to discover and to live what you have dreamed
  for me.

Lord, living in your grace, let me share a little, through the
  attention I give to others, your loving care for us.
Let me, on my knees, adore in them the mystery of your creative
  love.
Let me respect your idea of them without trying to impose my
  own.
May I allow them to follow the path that you have marked out
  for them without trying to take them along mine.
May I realize that they are indispensable to the world, and that I
  can't do without the least among them.
May I never tire of looking at them and of enriching myself with
  the treasures you have entrusted to them.
Help me to praise you in their journeying, to find you in their
  lives.
Grant that not an instant of their existence go by,
Not a hair of their heads fall,
By me, as by you, unheeded.

FOOTBALL AT NIGHT

Men would often rather be elsewhere, both in time and in space, than where they are, but this is a dangerous illusion. Each one is placed in the world in accordance with the Father's will for him. To make a success of one's life, and to help humanity to progress, one must take part in that life as fully as possible. That life is the work of the divine.

"Some he has appointed to be apostles, others to be prophets, others to be evangelists, or pastors, or teachers. They are to order the lives of the faithful, minister to their needs, build up the frame of Christ's body, until we all realize our common unity through faith in the Son of God. . . . On him all the body depends; it is organized and unified by each contact with the source which supplies it; and thus, each limb receiving the active power it needs, it achieves its natural growth, building itself up through charity." (Ephesians IV, 11, 16, KV)

This evening at the stadium the night was stirring, peopled with ten thousand shadows.

And when the projectors had painted green the velvet of the
great field,
The night intoned a choral, filled by ten thousand voices.

For the master of ceremonies had given the signal to begin the
service.
The impressive liturgy moved forward smoothly.
The ball flew from celebrant to celebrant,
As if everything had been minutely planned in advance.
It passed from hand to hand, slipped along the field, and flew
away overhead.
Each was at his post, taking the ball in turn, passing it to the
next one who was there to catch and pass again.
And because each one did his part—in the right place,
Because he put forth the effort required,
Because he knew he needed all the others,
Slowly but surely the ball gained ground
And made the final goal!

After the game, as the crowd flowed laboriously into the narrow
streets,
I reflected, Lord, that human history, for us a long game, is
for you this great liturgy,
A prodigious ceremony initiated at the dawning of time, which
will end only when the last celebrant has completed his
final rite.

In this world, Lord, we each have our place.
You, the far-sighted coach, have planned it for us.
You need us here, our brothers need us, and we need everyone.

94

It isn't the position I hold that is important, Lord,
But the reality and strength of my presence.
What difference whether I am a forward or a back, as long as I
    am fully what I should be?

Here, Lord, is my day before me. . . .

Did I sit too much on the sidelines, criticizing the play of others,
    my hands in my pockets?
Did I play my part well?
And when you were watching our side, did you see me there?
Did I catch my team-mate's pass and that of the player at the
    end of the field?
Did I co-operate with my team without seeking the limelight?
Did I play the game to win, and that each one should have a
    part in it?
Did I battle to the end in spite of setbacks, blows and bruises?
Was I troubled by the boos of the crowd, the muttering of the
    team, discouraged by their lack of understanding and their
    criticisms?
Made proud by their applause?
Did I think of praying my part, remembering that in the eyes of
    God this human game is the most religious of ceremonies?

I come in now to rest in the locker room, Lord.
Tomorrow, if you kick off, I'll play a new quarter,
And so each day . . .
Grant that this game, played with all my brothers, may be the
    imposing liturgy that you expect of us,
So that when your last whistle interrupts our lives, we shall be
    chosen for the prize of heaven.

LORD, I HAVE TIME

All men complain that they haven't enough time. They look at their lives from too human a point of view. There is always time to do what God wants us to do, but we must put ourselves completely into each moment that he offers us.

"Be most careful then how you conduct yourselves: like sensible men, not like simpletons. Use the present opportunity to the full, for these are evil days. So do not be fools, but try to understand what the will of the Lord is." (Ephesians V, 15-17)

I went out, Lord.
Men were coming and going,
Walking and running.

Everything was rushing: cars, trucks, the street, the whole town.
Men were rushing not to waste time.

96

They were rushing after time,
To catch up with time,
To gain time.

Good-bye, Sir, excuse me, I haven't time.
I'll come back, I can't wait, I haven't time.
I must end this letter—I haven't time.
I'd love to help you, but I haven't time.
I can't accept, having no time.
I can't think, I can't read, I'm swamped, I haven't time.
I'd like to pray, but I haven't time.

You understand, Lord, they simply haven't the time.
The child is playing, he hasn't time right now. . . . Later on. . . .
The schoolboy has his homework to do, he hasn't time. . . .
    Later on. . . .
The student has his courses, and so much work. . . . Later on. . . .
The young man is at his sports, he hasn't time. . . . Later on. . . .
The young married man has his new house; he has to fix it up.
    He hasn't time. . . . Later on. . . .
The grandparents have their grandchildren. They haven't
    time. . . . Later on. . . .
They are ill, they have their treatments, they haven't time. . . .
    Later on. . . .
They are dying, they have no. . . .
Too late! . . . They have no more time!

And so all men run after time, Lord.
They pass through life running—hurried, jostled, overburdened,
    frantic, and they never get there. They haven't time.
In spite of all their efforts they're still short of time,

Of a great deal of time.
Lord, you must have made a mistake in your calculations.
There is a big mistake somewhere.
The hours are too short,
The days are too short,
Our lives are too short.

You who are beyond time, Lord, you smile to see us fighting it.
And you know what you are doing.
You make no mistakes in your distribution of time to men.
You give each one time to do what you want him to do.
But we must not lose time
    waste time,
    kill time,
For time is a gift that you give us,
But a perishable gift,
A gift that does not keep.

Lord, I have time,
I have plenty of time,
All the time that you give me,
The years of my life,
The days of my years,
The hours of my days,
They are all mine.
Mine to fill, quietly, calmly,
But to fill completely, up to the brim,
To offer them to you, that of their insipid water
    You may make a rich wine such as you made once in Cana
    of Galilee.

I am not asking you tonight, Lord, for time to do this and then that,
But your grace to do conscientiously, in the time that you give me, what you want me to do.

THERE ARE TWO LOVES ONLY

We are made by love and for love. On earth we learn to love. At death we shall take our examination on love. If we have trained ourselves well enough, we shall live eternally in Love. Now, here below, every time that we love ourselves with a selfish love, we fail a little in carrying out God's plan for us and for the world. There are but two loves, love of ourselves and love of God and of others.

To live is to choose between these two loves.

"No servant can be slave to two masters; for either he will hate the first and love the second, or he will be devoted to the first and think nothing of the second." (Matthew VI, 24)

"Only the man who loves his brother dwells in light: there is nothing to make him stumble. But one who hates his brother is in darkness; he walks in the dark and has no idea where he is going, because the darkness has made him blind." (I John II, 10-11)

There are two loves only, Lord,
Love of myself and love of you and of others,
And each time that I love myself, it's a little less love for you and
    for others,
It's a draining away of love,
It's a loss of love,
For love is made to leave self and fly towards others.
Each time it's diverted to myself, it withers, rots and dies.
Love of self, Lord, is a poison that I absorb each day;
Love of self offers me a cigarette and gives none to my neighbor;
Love of self chooses the best part and keeps the best place;
Love of self indulges my senses and supplies them from the table
    of others;
Love of self speaks about myself and makes me deaf to the words
    of others;
Love of self chooses, and forces that choice on a friend;
Love of self puts on a false front; it wants me to shine, over-
    shadowing others;
Love of self is self-pitying and overlooks the suffering of others;
Love of self advertises my ideas and despises those of others;
Love of self thinks me virtuous, it calls me a good man;
Love of self induces me to make money, to spend it for my
    pleasure, to hoard it for my future;
Love of self advises me to give to the poor in order to ease my
    conscience and live in peace;
Love of self puts my slippers on and ensconces me in an easy
    chair;
Love of self is satisfied with myself; it gently rocks me to sleep.

What is more serious, Lord, is that love of self is a stolen love.
It was destined for others; they needed it to live, to thrive, and I
    have diverted it.
So the love of self creates human suffering,
So the love of men for themselves creates human misery,

All the miseries of men,
All the sufferings of men;

The suffering of the boy whose mother has slapped him without
cause and that of the man whose boss has reprimanded him
in front of the workers,
The suffering of the ugly girl neglected at a dance, and that of
the woman whose husband doesn't kiss her any more,
The suffering of the child left at home because he's a nuisance
and that of the grandfather made fun of because he's too
old,
The suffering of the worried man who hasn't been able to
confide in anyone and that of the troubled adolescent whose
worries have been ridiculed;
The suffering of the desperate man who jumps into the canal
and that of the criminal who is going to be executed,
The suffering of the unemployed man who wants to work and
that of the worker who ruins his health for a ridiculous
salary,
The suffering of the father who piles his family into a single
room next to an empty house and that of the mother whose
children are hungry while the remains of a party are thrown
into the garbage,
The suffering of one who dies alone, while his family, in the
adjoining room, wait for his death, drinking coffee.

All sufferings,
All injustices, bitternesses, humiliations, griefs, hates, despairs,
All sufferings are an unappeased hunger,
A hunger for love.
So men have built, slowly, selfishness by selfishness, a disfigured
world that crushes them;
So the men on earth spend their time feeding their self-love,

102

While around them others with outstretched arms die of hunger.
They have squandered love.
I have squandered your love, Lord.

Tonight I ask you to help me to love.

Grant me, Lord, to spread true love in the world.
Grant that by me and by your children it may penetrate a little
into all circles, all societies, all economic and political
systems, all laws, all contracts, all rulings;
Grant that it may penetrate into offices, factories, apartment
buildings, movie houses, dance halls;
Grant that it may penetrate the hearts of men and that I may
never forget that the battle for a better world is a battle of
love, in the service of love.

Help me to love, Lord,
    not to waste my powers of love,
    to love myself less and less in order to love others more and
    more,
That around me, no one should suffer or die because I have
stolen the love they needed to live.

Son, you will never succeed in putting enough love into the
heart of man and into the world,
For man and the world are hungry for an infinite love,
And God alone can love with a boundless love.
But if you want, son, I give you my Life,

Draw it within you.
I give you my heart, I give it to my sons.
Love with my heart, son,
And all together you will feed the world, and you will save it.

ALL

The Gospel preached in its utter purity exalts, frightens or shocks. It is bound to meet with violent reactions, as it is diametrically opposed to the standards of sinful men and of "the world." When a man really hears the Gospel, his whole life must be reassessed if he is sincere, for the demands of Christ do not admit half-measures.

"How blest you are, when you suffer insults and persecution and every kind of calumny for my sake. Accept it with gladness and exultation, for you have a rich reward in heaven. . . ." (Matthew V, 11-12)

"You must not think that I have come to bring peace to the earth; I have not come to bring peace, but a sword." (Matthew X, 34)

"If the world hates you, it hated me first, as you know well. If you belonged to the world, the world would love its own; but because you do not belong to the world, because I have chosen you out of the world, for that reason the world hates you. Re-

member what I said: 'A servant is not greater than his master. As
they persecuted me, they will persecute you. . . .'" (John XV,
18-20)

I heard a priest, one who lived the Gospel, preach the Gospel.
The humble, the poor, were carried away,
The prominent, the wealthy, were shocked.
And I thought that such preaching of the Gospel would soon
    frighten away many of those now filling the church, and
    attract those now shunning it.
It occurred to me that it is a bad sign for a follower of Christ to
    be well thought of by conventional "Christians."
Rather, it would be better if we were singled out as crazy or
    radical,
It would be better if they pursued us, signed petitions against us,
    tried to get rid of us.

This evening, Lord, I am afraid.
I am afraid, for your Gospel is terrible.
It is easy to hear it preached,
It is relatively easy not to be shocked by it,
But it is very difficult to live it.

I am afraid of deluding myself, Lord.
I am afraid of being satisfied with my decent little life,
I am afraid of my good habits, for I take them for virtues;
I am afraid of my little efforts, for I take them for progress;
I am afraid of my activities; they make me think I am giving
    myself.

106

I am afraid of my clever planning; I take it for success.
I am afraid of my influence; I imagine that it will transform
    lives;
I am afraid of what I give; it hides what I withhold;
I am afraid, Lord; there are people who are poorer than I;
Not so well educated,
    housed,
    heated,
    fed,
    cared for,
    loved.
I am afraid, Lord, for I do not do enough for them,
I do not do everything for them.

I should give everything,
I should give everything until there is not a single pain, a single
    misery, a single sin in the world.
I should then give all, Lord, all the time.
I should give my life.

Lord, it is not true, is it?
Your command is not for everyone—
I am exaggerating; I must be sensible!

Son, there is only *one* commandment,
For *everyone:*
You shall love with *all* your heart,
          with *all* your soul,
          with *all* your strength.

107

Stages of the Road

These prayers are not a spiritual treatise
on the Christian life. They merely describe
striking milestones in the lives of many
Christians. A collection of their expressions,
their words, is illuminating, and may help
others in communicating with God.

The first prayers are easy to grasp, but it
is not through the mind that the last can be
understood. It is only through life. Those
who haven't gone through these stages will
smile at the simplicity of the words, but
all those who have will relive in them their
own experience.

More prayers might have been written,
but they would have meaning for only a
few. It is enough to know that when a man
has decided to make room in his life for
God and his fellow men, the Lord never
ceases to teach him and help him to rise
above himself.

LORD, DELIVER ME
FROM MYSELF

There are men who are their own victims, more miserable than one can imagine because they are condemned to loving no one but themselves. One must understand their suffering to free them, for this suffering is nothing less than experiencing hell. If they find a friend who brings them to the realization that they are their own tormentors, it is the first step in their salvation; especially if they find a committed Christian who is to them the light and joy that can draw them away from themselves.

Perhaps then they will pray, "Lord, deliver me from myself." If they ask this earnestly, they are on the road to salvation. This is the first stage.

We too can say this prayer every night when we come home, to escape from ourselves to other men and to God.

"As he was starting out on a journey, a stranger ran up, and, kneeling before him, asked, 'Good Master, what must I do to win eternal life?'

". . . Jesus looked straight at him; his heart warmed to him, and he said, 'One thing you lack: go, sell everything you have, and give to the poor, and you will have riches in heaven; and come, follow me.' At these words his face fell and he went away

111

with a heavy heart; for he was a man of great wealth." (Mark X, 17, 21, 22)

Lord, do you hear me?

I'm suffering dreadfully,
Locked in myself,
Prisoner of myself.
I hear nothing but my own voice,
I see nothing but myself,
And behind me there is nothing but suffering.

Lord, do you hear me?

Deliver me from my body; it is all hunger, and everything it sees, everything its thousands of outstretched tentacles touch, is only something to be seized to satisfy its insatiable appetite.

Lord, do you hear me?

Deliver me from my heart; it is bursting with love; but then, just when I think that I love to the point of madness, I angrily perceive that it is still myself I am loving through the other one.

Lord, do you hear me?

Deliver me from my mind; it is full of itself, of its ideas, its
    opinions; it cannot carry on a dialogue, as no words reach
    it but its own.

Alone, I am bored,
    I am weary,
    I hate myself,
    I am disgusted with myself.
For ages I have been tossing and turning in my foul flesh like a
    man burning with fever in his sickbed.

Everything seems dark, ugly, horrid.
It's that I can look only through myself.
I feel ready to hate men and the whole world.
It's because I'm disappointed that I cannot love them.
I would like to get away,
Walk, run, to another land.
I know that joy exists; I have seen it on singing faces.
I know that light exists; I have seen it in radiant eyes.
But, Lord, I cannot get away, for I love my prison even while I
    hate it,
For my prison is myself,
And I love myself, Lord.
I both love and loathe myself.
Lord, I can no longer find the door of myself.
I grope around blindly,
I bump against the walls of my self, my own confines.
I hurt myself,
I am in pain,

I am in too much pain, and no one knows it, for no one has
   come in.
I am alone, all alone.

Lord, Lord, do you hear me?
Lord, show me my door,
      take me by the hand.
Open the door,
Show me the Way,
The path leading to joy, to light.

But . . .
But, Lord, do you hear me?

Son, I have heard you.
I am sorry for you.
I have long been watching your closed shutters. Open them;
   my light will come in.
I have long been standing at your locked door; open it; you will
   find me on the threshold.

I am waiting for you, the others are waiting for you,
But you must open,
You must come out.

Why choose to be a prisoner of yourself?
You are free.

114

It is not I who locked the door,
It is not I who can open it.
. . . For it is you, from the inside, who persist in keeping it firmly barred.

LORD, WHY DID
YOU TELL ME TO LOVE?

He who has begun to give himself to others is saved. In receiving his neighbor he will receive God and will be freed from himself. We are our own most deadly enemy. Humanly speaking, we bring suffering on ourselves, and supernaturally speaking we bar the road to God.

There are men who are bent on refining themselves. They examine themselves, spend their time combatting their faults, and never get beyond themselves, except sometimes to cultivate little hothouse virtues cut to their own size. They are wrong. Certain educators encourage them in this course, not realizing that by pointing out such and such a fault to conquer, such and such a quality to acquire, they center these persons' attention on self and condemn them to stagnation.

No, one should study men carefully to find out first, not what is bad in them but what is good, to discover their potentialities. Next, study in detail their environment and help them to become an integral part of it by giving themselves to others.

All men can and must give themselves. If they have one talent, let them give that; if they have ten, let them give the ten. It's only in giving that one can receive.

But anyone who has begun this giving realizes very quickly, if he is honest, that he can't retreat. He is afraid: one must then encourage him, show him that it's only on condition that he gives to others that he will succeed in his life and will know the joy of God.

116

"A long time afterwards their master returned, and proceeded to settle accounts with them. The man who had been given the five bags of gold came and produced the five he had made: 'Master,' he said, 'you left five bags with me; look, I have made five more.' 'Well done, my good and trusty servant!' said the master. 'You have proved trustworthy in a small way; I will now put you in charge of something big. Come and share your master's delight.' " (Matthew XXV, 19-21)

"It is by this that we know what love is: that Christ laid down his life for us. And we in our turn are bound to lay down our lives for our brothers. But if a man has enough to live on, and yet when he sees his brother in need shuts up his heart against him, how can it be said that the divine love dwells in him? My children, love must not be a matter of words or talk; it must be genuine, and show itself in action. This is how we may know that we belong to the realm of truth." (I John III, 16-19)

Lord, why did you tell me to love all men, my brothers?
I have tried, but I come back to you, frightened. . . .

Lord, I was so peaceful at home, I was so comfortably settled.
It was well-furnished, and I felt cozy.
I was alone, I was at peace,
Sheltered from the wind and the rain, kept clean.
I would have stayed unsullied in my ivory tower.

117

But, Lord, you have discovered a breach in my defenses.
You have forced me to open my door.
Like a squall of rain in the face, the cry of men has awakened me;
Like a gale of wind a friendship has shaken me,
Stealing in like a shaft of light, your grace has disturbed me.
Rashly enough, I left my door ajar. Now, Lord, I am lost!
Outside, men were lying in wait for me.
I did not know they were so near; in this house, in this street, in
this office; my neighbor, my colleague, my friend.
As soon as I started to open the door I saw them, with out-
stretched hands, anxious eyes, longing hearts, like beggars
on church steps.

The first came in, Lord. There was, after all, a bit of space in my
heart.
I welcomed them. I would have cared for them and fondled them,
my very own little lambs, my little flock.
You would have been pleased, Lord; I would have served and
honored you in a proper, respectable way.
Until then, it was sensible. . . .
But the next ones, Lord, the other men—I had not seen them;
they were hidden behind the first ones.
There were more of them. They were wretched; they overpowered
me without warning.
We had to crowd in, I had to find room for them.

Now they have come from all over in successive waves, pushing
one another, jostling one another.
They have come from all over town, from all parts of the country,
of the world; numberless, inexhaustible.
They don't come alone any longer but in groups, bound one to
another.

118

They come bending under heavy loads; loads of injustice, of re-
 sentment and hate, of suffering and sin. . . .
They drag the world behind them, with everything rusted,
 twisted, badly adjusted.

Lord, they hurt me! They are in the way, they are all over.
They are too hungry; they are consuming me!
I can't do anything any more; as they come in, they push the
 door, and the door opens wider. . . .
Ah, Lord! My door is wide open!
I can't stand it any more! It's too much! It's no kind of a life!
 What about my job?
 My family?
 My peace?
 My liberty?
 And me?
Ah, Lord! I have lost everything; I don't belong to myself any
 longer;
There's no more room for me at home.

Don't worry, God says, you have gained all,
While men came in to you,
I, your Father,
I, your God,
Slipped in among them.

HELP ME TO SAY "YES"

Marked by the joy of his first self-giving, the committed Christian can no longer retreat. Aroused by love, his emotions have helped him to surmount all obstacles. He is swept along, pushed along by those whose demands become more and more pressing. And now God appears, no longer hidden behind men but in full light. He asks to be received and given first place in man's life and activities. The Christian who has recognized him often runs away, for he knows that God will ask of him total and unconditional self-giving. Relentlessly the Lord pursues him to get the consent which will make his life divine.

Only those who have experienced this "wrestling" with God can really understand this prayer: "Help me to say 'Yes.'"

A painful stage; the educator, the friend, must understand it. Tactful—not to hinder God, *for he has himself just undertaken the training of his son*—but be *there* to enlighten through faith where needed: helping him to recognize the Lord, interpreting the questions which Love asks constantly through the events of life, pointing out his invitations, his advances, his wooing; he must encourage the Christian and urge him to say "Yes." If it hurts, it is because of his resistance; he must be helped to discover this. For one is always the loser when one strives with God. He is the stronger. His love is the stronger.

"Into her presence the angel came, and said, 'Hail, thou who art full of grace; the Lord is with thee'; . . . She was much perplexed at hearing him speak so, and cast about in her mind, what she was to make of such a greeting. Then the angel said to her, 'Mary, do not be afraid; thou hast found favour in the sight of God. And behold, thou shalt conceive in thy womb, and shalt bear a son, and shalt call him Jesus. He shall be great, and men will know him for the Son of the most High; . . . nothing can be impossible with God.' And Mary said, 'Behold the hand-maid of the Lord; let it be unto me according to thy word.'" (Luke I, 28-32, 37-38, KV)

I am afraid of saying "Yes," Lord.
Where will you take me?
I am afraid of drawing the longer straw,
I am afraid of signing my name to an unread agreement,
I am afraid of the "yes" that entails other "yeses."

And yet I am not at peace.
You pursue me, Lord, you besiege me.
I seek out the din for fear of hearing you, but in a moment of
    silence you slip through.
I turn from the road, for I have caught sight of you, but at the
    end of the path you are there awaiting me.
Where shall I hide? I meet you everywhere.
Is it then impossible to escape you?

But I am afraid to say "Yes," Lord.
I am afraid of putting my hand in yours, for you hold on to it.

I am afraid of meeting your eyes, for you can win me.
I am afraid of your demands, for you are a jealous God.
I am hemmed in, yet I hide.
I am captured, yet I struggle, and I fight knowing that I am
defeated.
For you are the stronger, Lord, you own the world and you take
it from me.
When I stretch out my hand to catch hold of people and things,
they vanish before my eyes.
It's no fun, Lord, I can't keep anything for myself.
The flower I pick fades in my hands.
My laugh freezes on my lips.
The waltz I dance leaves me restless and uneasy.
Everything seems empty,
Everything seems hollow,
You have made a desert around me.
I am hungry and thirsty,
And the whole world cannot satisfy me.

And yet I loved you, Lord; what have I done to you?
I worked for you; I gave myself for you.
O great and terrible God,
What more do you want?

Son, I want more for you and for the world.
Until now you have planned your actions, but I have no need
of them.
You have asked for my approval, you have asked for my support,
You have wanted to interest me in your work.
But don't you see, son, that you were reversing the roles?

122

I have watched you, I have seen your good will,
And I want more than you, now.
You will no longer do your own works, but the will of your
Father in heaven.

Say "Yes," son.
I need your "yes" as I needed Mary's "yes" to come to earth,
For it is I who must do your work,
It is I who must live in your family,
It is I who must be in your neighborhood, and not you.
For it is my look that penetrates, and not yours,
My words that carry weight, and not yours,
My life that transforms, and not yours.
Give all to me, abandon all to me.
I need your "yes" to be united with you and to come down to
earth,
I need your "yes" to continue saving the world!

O Lord, I am afraid of your demands, but who can resist you?
That your Kingdom may come and not mine,
That your will may be done and not mine,
Help me to say "Yes."

NOTHING, I AM NOTHING. . . .

Man does not know himself. No matter how carefully he examines his conscience, he finds there nothing very blameworthy. He is not humble. Try as he may to think poorly of himself, he never succeeds in destroying his self-esteem. At first the committed Christian, having left himself for others, finds success in his undertakings and gives himself credit for it. But in so doing he hinders God. It is only when man is deeply aware of his utter helplessness that God can begin to accomplish all.

Fortunately, when man effaces himself to make room for his brothers, God enters, and with him, his light. In this light he sees himself and the tiniest threads of his actions. He no longer needs to tell himself that it is God who directs his actions and makes them effective—*he knows it.*

The Christian must be urged not to shy away from this painful revelation, not to be discouraged, for this experience is a God-given grace, without which he would never have known the greatness of God and the smallness of man. May he never forget it.

"I am the vine, you are its branches; if a man lives on in me, and I in him, then he will yield abundant fruit; separated from me, you have no power to do anything." (John XV, 5, KV)

"Believe me when I tell you this; the man who has learned to believe in me will be able to do what I do; . . . and whatever request you make of the Father in my name, I will grant, so that through the Son the Father may be glorified. . . ." (John XIV, 12-13, KV)

Lord, you wanted it; here I am on the ground.
I don't even dare rise, I don't even dare look at you.
Nothing, I am nothing, I know it now.

Your light is terrible, Lord, and I'd like to escape it.
Since I have accepted you, your light has searched my dwelling.
Every day, mercilessly, you lay it bare,
And I see what I had never seen before.

I see the forest of my sins behind the tree that hid them.
I see innumerable roots, impossible to grasp.
I see that everything in me is an obstacle to you, as the smallest particle of matter blocks the sunlight and brings on the night.
I see the devil attacking the key points of the fortress that I thought impregnable, and I find myself tottering and ready to fall.
I see my helplessness, I, who thought that I could make myself of value to you.
I see that everything in me is mixed, and that not one of my actions is pure.
I see the infinite depth of each fault in the face of your infinite love.

125

I feel incapable of reaching a single soul through the noise of my
    words, and my gestures, beating the wind.
I see the Spirit blow where I haven't toiled, and the grain take
    root where I haven't sown.

Nothing, I am nothing; I accomplish nothing, I know it now.
Your light is hard, merciless, Lord.
No corner of my life, of my soul, remains in shadow.
Turn as I may, your light is everywhere,
And I stand naked and full of fear.

Formerly, I admitted that I was a sinner, that I was unworthy,
And I believed it, Lord, but I didn't understand it.
In your presence I looked for some faults
But produced only labored and feeble confessions.
Lord, it's my whole being that kneels now,
It's the sin that I *am* that asks forgiveness.

Lord, thank you for your light—I would never have known.
But, Lord, enough. I assure you I've understood.
I am nothing.
And you are all.

AGONY: LORD, I AM CRUSHED

The day will come when the committed Christian will experience a violent encounter with evil. In a few hours its depth and extent may be revealed to him. As he cannot communicate his secret to others, he will carry, crushed and alone, in revulsion and darkness, the evil he thought he knew, but of which he had seen only the fringes. This deep contact with the sin of the world is the first step in a trial which is essential to the purification of the Christian and to the deepening of his redemptive mission. This dark night will later settle in his innermost soul, but it will be the dawn of the resurrection.

"Christ never knew sin, and God made him into sin for us, so that in him we might be turned into the holiness of God." (II Corinthians V, 21, KV)

"And now he grew dismayed and distressed: 'My soul,' he said to them, 'is ready to die with sorrow; do you abide here, and keep watch.' So he went forward a little, and fell on the ground, and prayed that if it were possible, the hour might pass him by: 'Abba, Father,' he said, 'all things are possible to thee; take away this chalice from before me; only as thy will is, not as mine is.'" (Mark XIV, 33-36, KV)

"And now my soul is distressed. What am I to say? I will say, 'Father, save me from undergoing this hour of trial; and yet, I have only reached this hour of trial that I might undergo it. Father, make thy name known.'" (John XII, 27, 28, KV)

Lord, I am sickened,
 I am crushed tonight.
Sin is horrible, Lord,
 it is ugly,
 it is dirty.
I have walked in mud,
 traveled in mud,
 wallowed in mud.
The world is mud.

I feel that I must wash
 my hands,
 my eyes,
 my body,
 my heart,
 my soul,
 everything, Lord.
I've lost courage to go forward,
I hardly dare look at myself.
Why did you show me sin, why did you make me understand it?
 I can never forget it.
I feel so old tonight, older than my deceiving face.
In a few hours I have aged ten years.

128

Forgive me, Lord; I did not know.
Forgive the happy people, the sinless people, the pure, the
    innocent, who cannot understand, who will never know,
    never suspect, what sin is.
How hideous it is, Lord!

There is a picture before me: the smiling and honest face
    of a boy. And it both quiets and revolts me.
I envy him his innocence and I resent his calm.
I am drawn to his smile, yet it hurts me.
I crave his untarnished purity, yet it wounds me.
Lord, how know sin and yet remain pure?
How know, and be at peace?
How carry the infinite sadness of sin and keep within me your
    profound joy?

Son, you must accept this evil on your road;
    you must even carry it.
Don't stop, but seize it in passing;
    it's for this that I sent you treading these roads.
It crushes you. You can no longer go forward. You collapse, re-
    volted, in the dark, alone.
I know this;
I have experienced this, son.
That was my agony.
One must go through this; it's the law of my redemption.
For before rising one must die,
    and before dying one must suffer.
Don't run from evil; on the contrary, stay. Take hold of it.
The uglier it is, the heavier it is, the more firmly you must grasp

it;
and suffer,
and die.
Joy will follow.

TEMPTATION

When a Christian has chosen to live for God and for others, the devil is not pleased. At certain times the din of temptation, drowned out for a while by the song of love, returns more strident than ever.

God allows this trial and sometimes is even deaf to the appeals of his child, in order to test him and to bring him to greater trust. Only when the Christian expects nothing of himself and everything of God can he be at peace.

One must be very little to be carried by God.

"So he took ship, and his disciples followed him. And suddenly a great storm arose on the sea, so that the waves rose high over the ship; but he lay asleep. And his disciples came and roused him, crying, 'Lord, save us, we are sinking.' But Jesus said to them, 'Why are you faint-hearted, men of little faith?' Then he rose up, and checked the winds, and the sea, and there was deep calm." (Matthew VIII, 23-26, KV)

"Believe me, unless you become like little children again, you shall not enter the kingdom of heaven." (Matthew XVIII, 3, KV)

☆

I'm at the end of my rope, Lord.
I am shattered,
I am broken.
Since this morning I have been struggling to escape temptation,
   which, now wary, now persuasive, now tender, now sensuous,
   dances before me like a seductive girl at a fair.
I don't know what to do.
I don't know where to go.
It spies on me, follows me, engulfs me.
When I leave a room I find it seated and waiting for me in the
   next.
When I seize a newspaper, there it is, hidden in the words of
   some innocuous article.
I go out, and see it smiling at me on an unknown face.
I turn away and look at the wall, and it leaps at me from a poster.
I return to work, to find it dozing on my files, and when I gather
   my papers, it wakes up.
In despair, I take my poor head in my hands, I shut my eyes, to
   see nothing,
But I discover that it is more lively than ever, comfortably settled
   within me.
For it has broken my door open, it has slipped into my body,
   my veins,
      to the very tips of my fingers.
It has seeped into the crevices of my memory
And sings into the ear of my imagination.
It plays on my nerves as on the strings of a guitar.
I no longer know where I stand, Lord.
I no longer know whether or not I want this sin that beckons to
   me.
I no longer know whether I pursue it or am pursued.

132

I am dizzy, and the void draws me the way a chasm draws the rash
   mountaineer who can no longer either advance or retreat.
Lord, Lord, help me.

Son, I am here.
I haven't left you.
How weak your faith is!

You are too proud.
You still rely on yourself.
If you want to surmount all temptations, without falling or
   weakening, calm and serene,
You must surrender yourself to me.
You must realize that you are neither big enough nor strong
   enough;
You must let yourself be guided like a child,
My little child.

Come, give me your hand, and do not fear.
If there is mire, I will carry you in my arms.
But you must be very, very little,
For the Father carries only little children.

SIN

It is not only temptation that tries the generous Christian, but at times sin also; he may have a heavy fall, one that he had thought impossible, so deep and strong had seemed his love for the Lord. And having fallen, he is likely to become discouraged. Never before has he understood to such an extent the ugliness of sin— because he has now a greater understanding of the love of God.

All is grace. This fall will make him realize that he cannot rely on himself at all. It will put him in his place—at the bottom. But with this mistrust of himself must go a greater confidence in God, the Father.

"And indeed, for fear that these surpassing revelations should make me proud, I was given a sting to distress my outward nature, an angel of Satan sent to rebuff me. Three times it made me entreat the Lord to rid me of it; but he told me, My grace is enough for thee; my strength finds its full scope in thy weakness, . . . when I am weakest, then I am strongest of all." (II Corinthians XII, 7-10)

"So it is, I tell you, in heaven; there will be more rejoicing over one sinner who repents, than over ninety-nine souls that are justified, and have no need of repentance." (Luke XV, 7)

☆

I have fallen, Lord,
Once more.
I can't go on, I'll never succeed.
I am ashamed, I don't dare look at you.
And yet I struggled, Lord, for I knew you were right near me,
    bending over me, watching.
But temptation blew like a hurricane,
And instead of looking at you I turned my head away.
I stepped aside
While you stood, silent and sorrowful,
Like the spurned fiancé who sees his loved one carried away by
    the enemy.
When the wind died down as suddenly as it had arisen,
When the lightning ceased after proudly streaking the darkness,
All of a sudden I found myself alone, ashamed, disgusted, with
    my sin in my hands.

This sin that I selected the way a customer makes his purchase,
This sin that I have paid for and cannot return, for the store-
    keeper is no longer there,
This tasteless sin,
This odorless sin,
This sin that sickens me,
That I have wanted but want no more,
That I have imagined,
            sought,
            played with,
            fondled
    for a long time;
That I have finally embraced while turning coldly away from you,
My arms outstretched, my eyes and heart irresistibly drawn;

135

This sin that I have grasped and consumed with gluttony,
It's mine now, but it possesses me as the spider-web holds captive
the gnat.
It is mine,
It sticks to me,
It flows in my veins,
It fills my heart.
It has slipped in everywhere, as darkness slips into the forest at
dusk and fills all the patches of light.

I can't get rid of it.
I run from it the way one tries to lose a stray dog, but it catches
up with me and bounds joyfully against my legs.
Everyone must notice it.
I'm so ashamed that I feel like crawling to avoid being seen,
I'm ashamed of being seen by my friends,
I'm ashamed of being seen by you, Lord,
For you loved me, and I forgot you.
I forgot you because I was thinking of myself
And one can't think of several persons at once.
One must choose, and I chose.

And your voice
And your look
And your love hurt me.
They weigh me down
They weigh me down more than my sin.

Lord, don't look at me like that,
For I am naked,
I am dirty,
I am down,

Shattered,
With no strength left.
I dare make no more promises,
I can only lie bowed before you.

Come, son, look up.
Isn't it mainly your vanity that is wounded?
If you loved me, you would grieve, but you would trust.
Do you think that there's a limit to God's love?
Do you think that for a moment I stopped loving you?
But you still rely on yourself, son.
You must rely only on me.

Ask my pardon
And get up quickly.
You see, it's not falling that is the worst,
But staying on the ground.

IT IS DARK

It is only one totally blind who puts himself completely into the hands of God, to be led like a child. So, to raise the service of the Christian above the human level, the Lord is obliged to plunge him into darkness. He then learns to rely on God only.

He once had great faith in organized activities, and now he no longer knows what course to take. He once believed in the effectiveness of his words, and now he can no longer express himself. He once valued meetings, and now those he has carefully prepared fail dismally. Where he had met only with success, he now encounters only reverses. And God, seeming to make fun of his sudden and total ineffectiveness, acts along channels of his own without the help of this "useless servant." When the Christian, ashamed and in despair, turns to Christ to weep, he no longer finds him.

This is a painful time. The Christian mustn't try to escape it, but he does need to be reassured.

As the dam checks the flow of water to raise its level and unchain its power, so God, through outward failure, raises his disciple above the plane of mediocrity to a transcendence of self by faith.

*"When the sixth hour came, there was darkness over all the
earth until the ninth hour; and at the ninth hour Jesus cried out
with a loud voice, . . . 'My God, my God, why hast thou forsaken
me?' "* (Mark XV, 33-34, KV)

Lord, it is dark.
Lord, are you here in my darkness?

Your light has gone out, and so has its reflection on men and on
    all the things around me.
Everything seems grey and somber as when a fog blots out the sun
    and enshrouds the earth.
Everything is an effort, everything is difficult, and I am heavy-
    footed and slow.
Every morning I am overwhelmed at the thought of another day.
I long for the end, I yearn for the oblivion of death.
I should like to leave,
Run away,
Flee,
Anywhere, escape.
Escape what?
You, Lord, others, myself, I don't know,
But leave,
Flee.

I go along haltingly, like a drunkard,
From force of habit, unconsciously.
I go through the same motions each day, but I know that they
    are meaningless.

139

I walk, but I know that I am getting nowhere.
I speak, and my words seem dreadfully empty, for they can reach
 only human ears and not the living souls who are far above.
Ideas themselves escape me, and I find it hard to think.
I stammer, confused, blushing,
And I feel ridiculous
And abashed, for people will notice me.
Lord, am I losing my mind?
Or is all this what you want?

It wouldn't matter, except that I am alone.
I am alone.
You have taken me far, Lord; trusting, I followed you, and you
 walked at my side,
And now, in the middle of the desert, at night, suddenly you
 have disappeared.
I call, and you do not answer.
I search, and I do not find you.
I have left everything, and now am left alone.
Your absence is my suffering.

Lord, it is dark.
Lord, are you here in my darkness?
Where are you, Lord?
Do you love me still?
Or have I wearied you?
Lord, answer,
Answer!

It is dark.

LORD, YOU HAVE SEIZED ME

The Christian who has "capitulated" to the Lord, who has said "Yes," often receives his reward immediately. The Lord gives him the joy of possessing him and of being possessed by him.

Words are inadequate to describe this loving embrace of God. The boy who is "seized" by his Master right in the middle of the traffic, and has to dismount from his bicycle—suddenly unable safely to go on—will understand. So will the young girl who has to leave the workroom abruptly to hide from her companions her transfigured face. So, too, the boy who innocently confesses that he has to beg God to "leave him for a while" at a gathering in order to be available to his friends.

Though we must not seek these perceptible graces, we must be simple enough to thank the Lord when he grants them to us, enjoying his tenderness before experiencing his uncompromising firmness.

"... we have learned to recognize the love God has in our regard, to recognize it, and to make it our belief. God is love...."
(I John IV, 16, KV)

"That love resides, not in our showing any love for God, but in his showing love for us first. . . ." (I John IV, 10, KV)

"And all this, which once stood to my credit, I now write down as loss, for the love of Christ. For that matter, there is nothing I do not write down as loss compared with the high privilege of knowing Christ Jesus, my Lord; for love of him I have lost everything, treat everything else as refuse, if I may have Christ to my credit. . . . I only press on, in hope of winning the mastery, as Christ Jesus has won the mastery over me." (Philippians III, 7-8, 12, KV)

Lord, you seized me, and I could not resist you.
I ran for a long time, but you followed me.
I took bypaths, but you knew them.
You overtook me.
I struggled,
You won.
Here I am, Lord, out of breath, no fight left in me, and I've
    said "Yes" almost unwillingly.
When I stood there trembling like one defeated before his captor,
Your look of love fell on me.

The die is cast, Lord; I can no longer forget you.
In a moment you seized me,
In a moment you conquered me.
My doubts were swept away,
My fears dispelled.
For I recognized you without seeing you.

I felt you without touching you,
I understood you without hearing you.
Marked by the fire of your love, I can no longer forget you.
Now I know that you are there, close to me, and I work in peace
     beneath your gaze of love.
I no longer know what it is to make an effort to pray.
I just lift my eyes to you and I meet yours,
And we understand one another. All is light, all is peace.

At times, O Lord, you steal over me irresistibly, as the ocean
     slowly covers the shore,
Or suddenly you seize me as the lover clasps his beloved in his
     arms.
And I am helpless, a prisoner, and I have to stand still.
Captivated, I hold my breath; the world fades away, you suspend
     time.
I wish that these minutes were hours. . . .
When you withdraw, leaving me afire and overwhelmed with
     profound joy,
Though I have no new ideas, I know that you possess me more
     completely.
You have reached new depths in me,
The wound has widened, and I am more than ever a prisoner of
     your love.

Lord, once more you have made a desert around me, but this
     time it is different.
You are too great, you eclipse everything.
What I had cherished now seems trifling, and my desires melt
     like wax in the sun under the fire of your love.
Nothing matters to me,
Neither my comfort
Nor even my life.

143

I desire only you,
I want nothing but you

I know that the others say, "He is mad!"
But, Lord, it is they who are out of their minds.
They do not know you, they do not know God, they do not
    know that one cannot resist him.
But you have seized me, Lord, and I am sure of you
You are there, and I am overjoyed.
Sunlight floods over all, and my life shines like a jewel.
How easy everything is, how luminous!
All is pure and singing.

Thank you, Lord, thank you!
Why me, why did you choose me?
Joy, joy, tears of joy.

BEFORE YOU, LORD

Words, ideas, mental images are needed to nourish the beginner's prayers, but, little by little, he finds that all these props are obstacles in reaching God. Christ, when he takes hold of his disciple, makes him understand that it is useless for him to say or imagine or think anything at all. He must let God work in him. To expose oneself to him without intermediary is the surest way of meeting him when he calls. Nevertheless, receptivity does not mean forgetfulness of men. On the contrary, the disciple, laden with the weight of the brothers he has taken into his keeping, must bring them silently to God—in his presence, with them, to make possible a meeting.

"But when thou art praying, go into thy inner room and shut the door upon thyself, and so pray to thy Father in secret; and then thy Father, who sees what is done in secret, will reward thee.

*"Moreover, when you are at prayer, do not use many phrases.
..."* (Matthew VI, 6-7, KV)

"For my own part, I will gladly spend and be spent on your souls' behalf...." (II Corinthians XII, 15, KV)

"... no nursing mother ever cherished her children more; in our great longing for you, we desired nothing better than to offer you our own lives, as well as God's gospel, so greatly had we learned to love you." (I Thessalonians II, 7-8, KV)

To be there before you, Lord, that's all.
To shut the eyes of my body,
To shut the eyes of my soul,
And be still and silent,
To expose myself to you who are there, exposed to me.
To be there before you, the Eternal Presence.

I am willing to feel nothing, Lord,
　　to see nothing,
　　to hear nothing.
Empty of all ideas,
　　of all images,
In the darkness.
I am here as I am
To meet you without obstacles,
In the silence of faith,
Before you, Lord.

But, Lord, I am not alone,
I can no longer be alone.
I am a crowd, Lord,
For men live within me.
I have met them,

146

they have come in,
they have settled down,
they have worried me,
they have tormented me,
they have devoured me.
And I have allowed it, Lord, that they might be nourished and refreshed.
I bring them to you, too, as I come before you.
I expose them to you in exposing myself to you.
Here I am,
Here they are,
Before you, Lord.

Prayers on the Way
of the Cross

Christ is still dying. He continues to offer himself to his Father for the redemption of the world through the men who today suffer and die around us. The Way of the Cross is also the way to life; this a real Christian should never forget.

(I). JESUS IS CONDEMNED
TO DEATH

"So it was, brethren, that when I came to you and preached Christ's message to you, I did so without any high pretensions to eloquence, or to philosophy. I had no thought of bringing you any other knowledge than that of Jesus Christ, and of him as crucified. It was with distrust of myself, full of anxious fear, that I approached you; my preaching, my message depended on no persuasive language, devised by human wisdom, but rather on the proof I gave you of spiritual power; God's power, not man's wisdom, was to be the foundation of your faith." (I Corinthians II, 1-5, KV)

Lord, it's too late for you to be quiet, you have spoken too much;
    you have fought too much;
You were not sensible, you know, you exaggerated; it was bound
    to happen.
You called the better people a breed of vipers,
You told them that their hearts were black sepulchres with fine
    exteriors,
You chose the decaying lepers,
You spoke fearlessly with unacceptable strangers,

You ate with notorious sinners, and you said that streetwalkers would be the first in Paradise.

You got on well with the poor, the bums, the crippled.

You belittled the religious regulations.

Your interpretation of the Law reduced it to one little commandment: to love.

Now they are avenging themselves.

They have taken steps against you; they have approached the authorities, and action will follow.

Lord, I know that if I try to live a little like you, I shall be condemned.

I am afraid.

They are already singling me out.

Some smile at me, others laugh, some are shocked, and several of my friends are about to drop me.

I am afraid to stop,

I am afraid to listen to men's wisdom,

It whispers: you must go forward little by little, everything can't be taken literally, it's better to come to terms with the adversary. . . .

And yet, Lord, I know that you are right.

Help me to fight,

Help me to speak,

Help me to live your Gospel

To the end,

To the folly of the Cross.

152

(II). JESUS BEARS HIS CROSS

"If any man has a mind to come my way, let him renounce self, and take up his cross daily, and follow me. He who tries to save his life will lose it; it is the man who loses his life for my sake, that will save it." (Luke IX, 23-24, KV)

Lord, here is your Cross.

Your Cross! As if it were your cross!
You had no cross and you came to get ours, and all through
     your life, and along the way to Calvary, you took upon you,
     one by one, the sins of the world.
You have to go forward,
And bend,
And suffer.
The Cross must be carried.

Lord, you walk on silently; is it true, then, that there is a time
for speaking and a time for silence?
Is it true that there is a time for struggling and another for the
silent bearing of our sins and the sins of the world?

Lord, I would rather fight the Cross; to bear it is hard. The
more I progress, and the more I see the evil in the world, the
heavier is the Cross on my shoulders.
Lord, help me to understand that the most generous deed is nothing unless it is also silently redemptive.
And since you want for me this long way of the Cross,
At the dawning of each day, help me to set forth.

(III). JESUS FALLS
FOR THE FIRST TIME

*"Jesus said to them [Simon and Simon's brother Andrew],
'Come and follow me; I will make you into fishers of men.' And
they dropped their nets immediately, and followed him."* (Mark
I, 17-18, KV)

*"But Jesus said to them[James and John], 'Have you strength
to drink of the cup I am to drink of, to be baptized with the
baptism I am to be baptized with?' they said to him, 'We have.' "*
(Mark X, 38-39, KV)

*"But he took Peter and James and John with him. And now
he grew dismayed and distressed. . . . Then he went back, and
found them asleep; and he said to Peter, 'Simon, art thou sleeping? Hadst thou not strength to watch even for an hour?' "*
(Mark XIV, 33, 37, KV)

He fell.
For a moment he staggered, then fell prostrate,
God in the dust.

★

And so, Lord, I follow you, setting out with confidence, and now
    I have fallen.
I thought I had given myself irrevocably to you, but I caught
    sight of a flower on a foot-path.
I left you, I left the cumbersome Cross, and here I am off the
    road, possessed of a few faded petals and my solitude.
And the others, Lord, pass along the road, broken, exhausted,
And crosses are in the making and backs are bending.
I am no longer there to fight evil and to help men to drag their
    loads,
I am off the road.

Lord, help me not only to follow after you but to keep steadily
    on.
Keep me from sudden weaknesses that leave me stupefied and
    empty, far from the place where you are shaping the world.

(IV). JESUS MEETS HIS MOTHER

". . . as for thy own soul, it shall have a sword to pierce it."
(Luke II, 35, KV)

Lord, I pity your poor mother.
She follows,
She follows you,
She follows mankind on its Way of the Cross.

She walks in the crowd, unknown, but she doesn't take her eyes
    off you.
Every gesture of yours, every sigh, every blow dealt you, every
    wound, pierces her heart.
She knows your sufferings,
She suffers your sufferings,
And without coming near you,
    without touching you,
    without speaking to you,
Lord, with you she saves the world.

Often, mingled with the crowd, I accompany men on their Way of the Cross,

And I am crushed by evil.

I feel incapable of saving the world; it is too heavy and rotten, and every day at the turn of the road I become acquainted with new injustices and new impurities.

Lord, show me your mother Mary,

The useless one, the ineffectual one in the sight of men,

But the co-redemptrix in the sight of God.

Help me to walk among men, eager to know their miseries and their sins.

May I never avert my eyes,

May I never close my heart, that in welcoming the sufferings of the world, with Mary, your mother, I may suffer and redeem.

(V). SIMON OF CYRENE
HELPS CARRY JESUS' CROSS

"... *and led him away to be crucified. As for his cross, they forced a passer-by who was coming in from the country to carry it, one Simon of Cyrene....*" (Mark XV, 20-21, KV)

"*Bear the burden of one another's failings; then you will be fulfilling the law of Christ.*" (Galatians VI, 2, KV)

He passed by on the road;
They pressed him into service,
The first to come along, a stranger.

Lord, you accepted his help.
You did not want the help of a friend, the solace of a gesture of
    love, the generous impulse of one who cared.
You chose the enforced help of an indifferent and timid fellow.
Lord All-Powerful, you sought the help of a powerless man.
By your own choosing you are in need of us.

Lord, I need others.

The way of man is too hard to be trodden alone.

But I avoid the hands outstretched to help me,

I want to act alone,

I want to fight alone,

I want to succeed alone.

And yet beside me walk a friend, a spouse, a brother, a neighbor, a fellow-worker.

You have placed them near me, Lord, and too often I ignore them.

And yet it is together that we shall save the world.

Lord, even if they are requisitioned, grant that I may see, that I may accept, all the Simons on my road.

(VI). A WOMAN WIPES
THE FACE OF JESUS

*"We carry about continually in our bodies the dying state of
Jesus, so that the living power of Jesus may be manifested in our
bodies too."* (II Corinthians IV, 10, KV)

*"At present, we are looking at a confused reflection in a mir-
ror; then, we shall see face to face. . . ."* (I Corinthians XIII, 12,
KV)

For a long time, Lord, her eyes were on you;
She suffered from your suffering.
Unable to bear it any longer, she pushed the soldiers aside, and
     with a cloth of fine linen wiped your face.
Were your bleeding features imprinted on her cloth? Maybe.
In her heart, surely.

Lord, I needed to contemplate you at great length, disinter-
     estedly, as a little brother admires and loves his big brother.

161

For I want to resemble you; and for that I must first look at you.

If you want, I shall become a little like you, since friends who love each other become one.

But, Lord, too often I carelessly pass in front of you, or am bored when I stop and look at you.

And to others I must be a sad caricature of you.

Forgive my body, eager for pleasures: it does not bring your presence to others.

Forgive my clouded eyes: in them others cannot see your light.

Forgive my encumbered heart: in it others do not see your love.

Nevertheless, Lord, come to me; my door is open

(VII). JESUS FALLS
FOR THE SECOND TIME

". . . they all grew drowsy, and fell asleep." (Matthew XXV,
5, KV)
*"Only look well to yourselves; do not let your hearts grow
dull. . . . Keep watch, then, praying at all times, so that you may
be found worthy to come safe through all that lies before you, and
stand erect to meet the presence of the Son of Man."* (Luke XXI,
34, 36, KV)

Lord, you are spent.
Again you have fallen to the ground.
This time you fall not only from the weight of the Cross but
from exhaustion.

Recurrent suffering numbs the will.
My sins, Lord, are dulling my conscience.
I get used to evil very quickly:
A little self-indulgence here,

A small unfaithfulness there,
An unwise action further on,
And my vision becomes obscured; I no longer see stumbling-
blocks, I no longer see other people on my road,

My ears gradually close; I no longer hear the complaints of men.
I find myself on the ground, on the plain, far from the road
you laid out for me.

Lord, I beseech you, keep me young in my efforts,
Spare me the bondage of habit, which lulls to sleep and kills.

(VIII). JESUS REBUKES
THE DAUGHTERS OF JERUSALEM

*"How is it that thou canst see the speck of dust which is in
thy brother's eye, and art not aware of the beam which is in thy
own? By what right wilt thou say to thy brother, 'Brother, let
me rid thy eye of that speck,' when thou canst not see the beam
that is in thy own? Thou hypocrite, take the beam out of thy
own eye first, and so thou shalt have clear sight to rid thy
brother's of the speck."* (Luke VI, 41-42, KV)

They weep.
They sob.
It's easy to understand if you see what men have done to him.
And they are helpless, they cannot interfere,
So they weep, they weep in pity.

Lord, you have seen them, you have heard them,
But you said: "Weep first for *your* sins."

To pity your sufferings and the sufferings of the world I manage
very well, Lord,
But to weep for my own sins, that's another matter.
I'd as lief bemoan those of others,
It's easier.
I'm well up on that; the whole world passes every day before
my tribunal.
I've found plenty of guilt: in politics, economics, slums, alcohol,
movies, industry. I see it in many people: in laissez-faire
Christians, in priests who don't understand a thing, and in
many others, Lord, many others.
All in all, in just about the whole world save me.

Lord, teach me that I am a sinner.

166

(IX). JESUS FALLS
FOR THE THIRD TIME

"Jesus said to him, 'Believe me, this night, before the cock crows, thou wilt thrice disown me.'" (Matthew XXVI, 34, KV)

"Peter was deeply moved when he was asked a third time, 'Dost thou love me?' and said to him, 'Lord, thou knowest all things; thou canst tell that I love thee.'" (John XXI, 17, KV)

Again.
You do not move, for all the soldiers' beating.
Lord, are you dead?
No, but utterly spent.
A minute of terrible anxiety.
But you begin again, just as you are, Lord, and walk on. One
step, then another . . .
Lord, you have fallen a third time, but this time close to Calvary.

Again.

I fall every time.

I'll never get there.

But I've said that before, Lord, and please forgive me, for you
were right with me, you were just testing my trust.

If I become discouraged, I am lost.

If I keep up the fight, I am saved.

For you fell a third time, but you had nearly reached Calvary.

(X). JESUS IS STRIPPED
OF HIS GARMENTS

"The time has come now for the Son of Man to achieve his glory. Believe me when I tell you this; a grain of wheat must fall into the ground and die, or else it remains nothing more than a grain of wheat; but if it dies, then it yields rich fruit." (John XII, 23-24, KV)

You had nothing left but your own cloak;
You were fond of it, your Mother had woven it for you.
But this, too, had to go.
One thing only is needful, Lord, your Cross.

Nothing comes now between you and the Cross;
You are finally going to be united forever,
And together you will save the world.

And so, Lord, I must give up all these trappings which hinder me and hide me from your sight.

169

This "possessing" which stifles the "being" in me and separates me from others.

Thus, Lord, little by little all in my life must die which is not an expression of your will.

I don't like it, Lord. It's always a question of dying!

How demanding you are!

I give, and you want more.

I'd like to keep a few trifles,

A few trifles I cling to and can't bring myself to offer you.

· · · · · · · · · ·

But if you want all, Lord, take all.

Strip me, yourself, of my last garment.

For I well know that we must die to deserve life,

As the seed must die to yield the golden grain.

170

(XI). JESUS IS NAILED
TO THE CROSS

"... with Christ I hang upon the cross, and yet I am alive; or rather, not I; it is Christ that lives in me. True, I am living, here and now, this mortal life; but my real life is the faith I have in the Son of God, who loved me, and gave himself for me." (Galalations II, 19-20, KV)

Lord, you stretch at full length on the Cross.
There.
Without a doubt, it is made for you.
You cover it entirely, and to adhere to it more surely, you allow
    men to nail you carefully to it.
Lord, it was work well done, conscientiously done.
Now you fit your Cross exactly, as the mechanic's carefully filed
    parts fit the engineer's blueprint.
There had to be this precision.

Thus, Lord, I must gather my body, my heart, my spirit,
And stretch myself at full length on the Cross of the present moment.
I haven't the right to choose the wood of my passion.
The Cross is ready, to my measure.
You present it to me each day, each minute, and I must lie on it.
It isn't easy. The present moment is so limited that there is no room to turn around.
And yet, Lord, I can meet you nowhere else.
It's there that you await me.
It's there that together we shall save our brothers.

(XII). JESUS DIES
ON THE CROSS

"... *he dispossessed himself, and took the nature of a slave,
fashioned in the likeness of men, and presenting himself to us
in human form; and then he lowered his own dignity, accepted
an obedience which brought him to death, death on a cross.*"
(Philippians II, 7-8, KV)

"... *we too must be ready to lay down our lives for the sake
of our brethren.*" (I John III, 16, KV)

A few hours more,
A few minutes more,
A few instants more.
For thirty-three years it has been going on.
For thirty-three years you have lived fully minute after minute.
You can no longer escape, now; you are there, at the end of
  your life, at the end of your road.
You are at the last extremity, at the edge of a precipice.
You must take the last step,
The last step of love,
The last step of life that ends in death.

173

You hesitate.
Three hours are long, three hours of agony;
Longer than three years of life,
Longer than thirty years of life.

You must decide, Lord, all is ready around you.
You are there, motionless, on your Cross.
You have renounced all activity other than embracing these
    crossed planks for which you were made.
And yet, there is still life in your nailed body.
Let mortal flesh die, and make way for Eternity.

Now, life slips from each limb, one by one, finding refuge in his
    still-beating heart,
Immeasurable heart,
Overflowing heart,
Heart heavy as the world, the world of sins and miseries that it
    bears.

Lord, one more effort.
Mankind is there, waiting unknowingly for the cry of its Saviour.
Your brothers are there; they need you.
Your Father bends over you, already holding out his arms.
Lord, save us,
Save us.

See.
He has taken his heavy heart.
And
Slowly,
Laboriously,

174

Alone between heaven and earth,
In the awesome night,
With passionate love,
He has gathered his life,
He has gathered the sin of the world,
And in a cry,
He has given ALL.
"Father, into thy hands I commend my spirit."

Christ has just died for us.

Lord, help me to die for you.
Help me to die for them.

(XIII). JESUS IS GIVEN
TO HIS MOTHER

"... *and his mother said to him, 'My Son, why hast thou treated us so? Think, what anguish of mind thy father and I have endured, searching for thee.' But he asked them, 'What reason had you to search for me? Could you not tell that I must needs be about my Father's business?'*" (Luke II, 48-49, KV)

Your work is done,
You can leave your Cross,
You can come down to rest, you have surely earned it.

Slowly you slip down, like a man weary of labor and drowsy with sleep.
Your mother takes you in her arms.
You rest in peace.
Over your face, calm and serene, there passes a ray of joy. All is accomplished.
You have made your mother suffer, but she is proud of you
"Sleep now, my little one, your Mother is watching you."

176

☆

Thus each night, my day ended, I fall asleep.
What a state I am in sometimes, Lord.
But, alas, it is not always in serving the Father that I have become soiled and tired.
Mary, will you be willing, even so, to watch over me every night?
My body is weighed down with its failures, but my heart asks forgiveness.
Don't forget, you are the refuge of sinners.

Holy Mary, Mother of God, pray for me, a poor sinner.
Grant that through the merits of your Son, I may never fall asleep without receiving the forgiveness of our Father,
That, each night, resting in peace in your arms, I may learn how to die.

(XIV). JESUS IS LAID
IN THE TOMB

*". . . in this mortal frame of mine, I help to pay off the debt
which the afflictions of Christ still leave to be paid, for the sake
of his body, the Church."* (Colossians I, 24, KV)

*"The sufferings of Christ, it is true, overflow into our lives;
but there is overflowing comfort, too, which Christ brings to us."*
(II Corinthians I, 5, KV)

Let's forget it now,
And all go home.
He is buried and the stone is in place.
His family is in tears, his friends are lost.
This time it is really over.

Lord, it is not over.
"You are in agony till the end of time,' I know.

178

Men tread in relays the Way of the Cross.

The resurrection will only be completed when they have reached the end of the Way.

I am on the road; I have a small share of your suffering and the others have theirs.

Together we help you to carry the burden that you have assumed and made divine.

There lies my hope, Lord, and my invincible trust.

There is not a fraction of my little suffering that you have not already lived and transformed into infinite redemption.

When the road is hard and monotonous,

When it leads to the grave,

I know that beyond the grave you are waiting for me in your glory.

Lord, help me faithfully to travel along my road, at my proper place in the vastness of humanity.

Help me above all to recognize you and to help you in all my pilgrim brothers.

For it would be a lie to weep before your lifeless image if I did not follow you, living, on the road that men travel.